Breaking the Confines

The Grand Tour

Breaking the Confines

Flavio Conti

Translated by Patrick Creagh

HBJ Press
a subsidiary of Harcourt Brace Jovanovich, Inc.
Boston

HBJ Press

President, Robert J. George

Publisher, Giles Kemp

Vice President, Richard S. Perkins, Jr.

Managing Director, Valerie S. Hopkins

Executive Editor, Marcia Heath

Series Editor, Carolyn Hall

Staff Editor, Chris Heath

Text Editors: Leonard Bushkoff, Elizabeth S. Duvall, Judith E. Hanhisalo, Amanda Heller, Joyce Milton

Editorial Production: Karen E. English, Ann McGrath, Eric Brus, Betsie Brownell, Patricia Leal, Pamela George

Project Coordinator, Linda S. Behrens

Business Manager, Edward Koman

Marketing Director, John R. Whitman

Public Relations, Janet Schotta

Business Staff: Pamela Herlich, Joan Kenney

Architectural Consultant, Dennis J. DeWitt

Text Consultants: Janet Adams, Elizabeth R. DeWitt, Perween Hasan

Design Implementation, Designworks

Rizzoli Editore

Authors of the Italian Edition: Dr. Flavio Conti, P. Favole, G. Gattoni, G. M. Tabarelli

Idea and Realization, Harry C. Lindinger

General Supervisor, Luigi U. Re

Graphic Designer, Gerry Valsecchi

Coordinator, Vilma Maggioni

Editorial Supervisor, Gianfranco Malafarina

Research Organizer, Germano Facetti

U.S. Edition Coordinator, Natalie Danesi Murray

Photography Credits:

Australian Embassy in Rome: pp. 153–157, 160–163 / *Borromeo:* p. 28, p. 29 above, p. 63 below / *Carrese:* p. 115 below / *Charbonnier:* p. 32 / *Chiappa:* p. 108 below right / *Coradeschi:* p. 48 below left, p. 49 / *Costa:* p. 12, p. 13 below, pp. 15–16. p. 23 / *Forman:* p. 29 below left and right / *Hutchinson:* p. 50 right / *Magnum-Barbey:* p. 41, p. 45, p. 114 above left and center right, p. 114 below right, p. 115 above / *Magnum-Burri:* p. 31, pp. 42–43, pp. 46–47, p. 51 above, p. 79, p. 77 below, p. 88 above and below, p. 91, p. 92 right, p. 92 above left, p. 95 left, p. 95 below right, p. 105, p. 108 above center and bottom left, pp. 109–113, p. 114 below left, p. 116 / *Magnum-Riboud:* p. 50 above left / *Magnum-Rodger:* p. 57, p. 63 above left, p. 64, pp. 67–68 / *Marka:* pp. 106–107 / *Maurituis:* pp. 80–81, p. 96 / *Mohr J.:* p. 63 center, p. 66 below / *Publifoto-Kessel:* pp. 86–87, p. 88 center, pp. 89–90, p. 92 below left, pp. 93–94, p. 95 above and center right / *Ricciarini:* p. 14, p. 22 above / *S.E.F.:* p. 17, p. 76 below / *Sheridan:* pp. 24–25, p. 73, p. 76 above / *SIPA Press:* pp. 26–27, p. 48 above left, p. 50 below left / *Sirtori:* p. 13 above and center, p. 30 / *Stern:* pp. 10–11, pp. 74–75, p. 78 / *Stierlin:* p. 9, pp. 18–19, p. 20 top, p. 22 bottom, pp. 58–62, p. 63 above right, p. 64 above, p. 65, p. 66 above, p. 77 above, p. 79 below left and right, pp. 82–85 / *Taborri-Soave:* pp. 158–159 / *Rizzoli:* p. 20 below, p. 21, p. 52, p. 121, pp. 124–132 / *Verg:* p. 44, p. 48 above right, p. 164 / *Visalli:* pp. 122–123, pp. 137–148.

Library of Congress Catalog Card Number: 78–56251
ISBN: 0–15–003730–9

Printed in Hong Kong by Mandarin Publishers Limited

Contents

Preface

Breaking the Confines

Mankind is continually changing and reshaping the world through architecture. Every road, house, or bridge we build alters the human environment and has its effect—however small—on the lives and souls of those who see it or live in it.

Most architects or builders are constrained by the mundane pressures of time, money, and conservative clients. Most often, they are given bread-and-butter commissions to design buildings that are simply functional without being dramatically innovative, monumental, or beautiful. But on rare occasions an architect is given the opportunity to explore new possibilities, to put into practice new ideas, discoveries, and methods, to create a bigger or more beautiful building than has ever been built before. He is challenged to produce a work of monumental proportions which also demands a rigorous technical excellence. And sometimes he not only meets such a challenge but, in so doing, also creates a masterpiece, which then finds itself a niche in the history of architecture.

Many people, however, confuse greatness with size and admire bigness for its own sake, sometimes valuing it over quality or execution. Apparently, this has always been the case. The Acropolis, for all its purity of proportions, did not figure among the Seven Wonders of the World. Yet among these wonders were two gigan-

tic statues—the Colossus of Rhodes, a statue probably a hundred feet tall, which stood at the entrance to the harbor of Lindos, and the statue of Zeus, also prodigiously large, which the Greek sculptor Phidias made for the Temple of Zeus at Olympia. Both statues are lost, but all accounts of them tellingly dwell on their size rather than their beauty.

But there are exceptions. Also numbered among the Seven Wonders of the World—again because of their sheer size— were the Great Pyramids of Egypt. Probably no other structures in the world can rival their combination of extreme mass and extreme simplicity of form. For centuries their huge enigmatic presence has challenged man's need to explain and understand: They have been classified, more or less sensibly, not only as tombs but also as shrines, theorems in stone, cosmic machines, and vast esoteric symbols. Yet little is known even now about the meanings of these monuments or the identity of their ancient builders. Today the Pyramids still dominate the Giza plain, as they have for almost five millenniums, and continue to guard their secrets well.

Other monuments of ancient Egypt have also warranted their place in this volume. Here are the immense temples at Abu Simbel. Carved in the living rock, they were commissioned by the prolific builder Rameses II, whose colossal like-

nesses overlook the life-giving waters of the Nile. And like the temples on the island sanctuary of Philae, these monuments have earned recognition twice over: first, for the skill of their original builders and second, for the technology that rescued them from the newly dammed waters of the Nile. The entire cliff face that contained the temples at Abu Simbel was cut apart in twenty-ton blocks and reassembled against a manmade hill above the new level of the river. The Temple of Isis was also dismantled and relocated on a higher nearby island. At once massive and delicate, these modern-day reconstructions are more difficult than the original construction of the temples—as well as staggeringly expensive.

Perhaps more than any other age in history, ours appreciates those works of architecture which exhibit some special combination of technical innovation and grandiose proportions—perhaps because requirements of our century and the new techniques it has discovered have led to many achievements of this kind.

A classic example, the Empire State Building, is known the world over as the archetypal skyscraper. It is also a symbol of America itself. Constructed during the worst economic crisis in the history of the United States, it nevertheless represented all the technology, pride, and resources of the country and was for forty years the tallest building in the world. It cannot be termed an aesthetic masterpiece—its design is rather conventional—but it is clearly a feat of engineering on a heroic scale. And its mystique endures. Le Corbusier himself was apparently overcome by its size. He claimed that, when he first saw it, he wanted to lie down on the sidewalk and gaze up at it forever.

The Golden Gate Bridge also held a title for many years after it was built. A magically airy bridge joining San Francisco to Marin County across the strait known as the Golden Gate, it was from 1937 to 1965 the longest suspension bridge in the world. And it may well remain the most beautiful. A pure expression of function, stated with an unparalleled eloquence and conviction, its cables sweep weightlessly across the water in an elusive harmony of sky, sea, and steel.

The ocean, most obvious as a backdrop for bridges, can also enhance and complement buildings. The new Opera House in Sydney, Australia, is a case in point. Dramatically poised between the southern sky and the sea, visible from all angles, it is constructed on a small peninsula in Sydney Harbour. Its architect, the Danish-born Jørn Utzon, aspired to create a building which would be worthy of its stunning location. His design proved to be a continual challenge to the technical possibilities of the materials, and his original idea had to be modified repeatedly. Today the sails of the Opera House make it the only Australian building known throughout the world. But such a human and technical adventure has a price—a price not only calculated in millions of dollars but also exacted in human jealousies, disagreements, misunderstandings, bitterness, and humiliations.

Some technical innovations are not inherently beautiful. The funicular which climbs Sugar Loaf Mountain in Rio de Janeiro, for example, is in itself unremarkable, but it does afford a magnificent view of the city and its beaches, of Corcovado with its huge figure of Christ, of the bay and its islands. The conical Sugar Loaf is perhaps the best-known landmark in Rio. Like a huge eighteenth-century loaf of sugar, it towers 1,300 feet at the entrance to Guanabara Bay, a welcome beacon for sailors and city folk alike.

If it were only for its length, the Great Wall of China would earn a place as the world's most conspicuous landmark. Over 3,500 miles in length, the Great Wall is claimed to be the only work of mankind which would be visible from the moon—although this has never been verified. Like the Pyramids of Giza, the scale of the project demanded an unprecedented number of laborers—countless numbers of whom perished during its construction. The wall, commissioned by the despotic Emperor Shih Huang Ti, formed both a geographic and cultural barrier, separating the civilized world from the darkness beyond. As such, it symbolized the hopes and fears, indeed the whole character, of the Chinese people.

The smallest of all the monuments in this volume is the observatory of the Maharajah Jai Singh II of Jaipur in India. Yet the astronomical instruments built by this Indian prince early in the eighteenth century are huge in comparison with those in use at the time. Jai Singh attempted to improve upon the precision of those instruments by building his own on a larger scale. Although his geometric stone constructions were disappointing as a scientific experiment, they are now appreciated as architectural curiosities, poetic statements in their own right—and are strangely reminiscent of the best abstract sculpture of the twentieth century.

The monuments in this volume are a few of the most dramatic and technically innovative works of architecture in the world—milestones in architectural history. As exciting today as when they were first built, they remain an inspiration to the creativity and ambitions of succeeding generations.

The Great Pyramids at Giza

Egypt

Preceding page, the Giza necropolis, established by Cheops, the most important of the six pharaohs of Egypt's Fourth Dynasty. The Great Pyramid of Cheops on the right and the slightly smaller one of his son Chephren represent the apogee of the pyramid form, the grandest of about eighty such monuments built before the rulers of Egypt turned to less imposing but more secure forms of funerary architecture. These manmade mountains dominate the Giza landscape, testifying to the supreme power of the pharaohs.

Many court functionaries and lesser members of the royal family were also entombed here. Three small pyramids, just discernible in the shadows to the right of the Great Pyramid of Cheops, housed the remains of that pharaoh's wives. Eight double mastabas, or flat-topped tombs, seen in front of the pyramid beside an excavated funeral boat were built for his favorite children. At the end of the long causeway, which stretches from the Pyramid of Chephren and past some minor tombs, are the Sphinx and restored Valley Temple where Chephren's mummy was prepared for its "house of eternity." Ruins of a comparable causeway and temple attached to the Great Pyramid have never been excavated because they lie under an adjacent modern village.

From earliest times, Egyptian civilization has been concentrated around a narrow strip of land annually inundated by the flooding Nile. Left, lush fields on the banks of the sacred river, only a few yards from the desert sands of Giza and the stark silhouettes of the pyramids.

In this valley the rhythms of agriculture changed little over the milleniums—until the damming of the Nile at Aswan upset the natural cycle of flooding and silting which made this land so fertile. For the present, the soil is still rich (bottom right), and farmers continue to depend on the Nile for irrigation of their fields (center right).

Left, the three major pyramids of Giza. To the left is the Pyramid of Mycerinus and in front of it the much smaller tomb of his queen Khamerernebti II. Two other wives of this pharaoh were buried in small pyramids whose ruins lie nearby. Mycerinus, the son of Chephren and grandson of Cheops, had intended to have his tomb finished with a commanding façade of blood-red Aswan granite. Unfortunately, he died young and his pyramid was hastily finished with plain mud bricks. Although the sides of its square base measure approximately 356 feet, it covers only one quarter of the area of Cheops's monument. The reign of Mycerinus appears to have been a troubled one. He was challenged by rival lines of his grandfather's family, and by the time of his death, the power of the rulers of the Fourth Dynasty had diminished considerably. However, two famous slate statues, now in the Boston Museum of Fine Arts, show a happier aspect of Mycerinus' reign. In an apparent departure from the tradition of representing the rulers alone, the statues show Queen Khamerernebti standing with her arm placed affectionately around the waist of the young pharaoh.

An ancient symbol of inscrutability, the 66-foot tall Sphinx (above) has intrigued visitors since Roman times. Carved out of a rocky outcrop which had been left behind during quarrying operations for the Great Pyramids, the figure represents a man's head joined to the body of a lion. Herodotus did not mention the Sphinx, perhaps because it was hidden by drifting sand at the time of his visit. The archaeologist Dr. George A. Reisner concluded that the massive head was a portrait of Chephren and that the function of the Sphinx was to guard the pharaoh's remains.

The Great Pyramid of Cheops (above left) is the most massive masonry structure ever built. It was originally 480 feet tall, but over the centuries its summit has eroded some 30 feet. Crews of about 4,000 men at a time labored without benefit of winches, pulleys, or wheels to raise over 2,300,000 stone blocks weighing between two and fifteen tons each. Left, the restored façade of a funerary temple which stands at the base of the pyramid. Just behind it lie the remains of the three small pyramidal tombs of the pharaoh's wives.

Right, the Pyramid of Chephren. Both the pyramids of Cheops and Chephren were once sheathed with polished Tura limestone, but today only a remnant of this remains on the upper reaches of Chephren's monument. In the foreground is a modern Arab cemetery.

Although Chephren's pyramid (foreground, preceding page) appears to dominate its larger neighbor, its sides measure only 708 feet compared with the 756-foot sides of his father's pyramid—Chephren cleverly placed his on a higher, more prominent site.

The monumental tombs of the pharaohs of the Fourth Dynasty were intended to last for eternity. Indeed, they have stood for forty-six centuries. The main entrance on the north side of the Great Pyramid (right) was meant to be sealed for all time. Just below this limestone door, a tour guide waits to usher visitors through a rough hole that was opened during the ninth century A.D. by the Caliph Mamun. The tombs had previously been opened and resealed several times, and whatever treasures they once contained were rifled thousands of years ago.

Left, a group of Arabs resting before the Great Pyramid.

Despite its apparent serenity, the Sphinx has endured much adversity from both man and nature. French scholars who came to Egypt with Napoleon's army found the Sphinx buried up to its neck in sand; a protective wall erected in the second century A.D. had failed to stop the accumulating drifts. The figure was dug free in 1818 and once again in 1886. The image of the Sphinx in Western literature as a poser of riddles led one Englishman, Richard Howard-Vyse, to hypothesize that the statue was hollow so that it could amplify the voices of priests delivering oracles. Howard-Vyse bored large holes into its side but failed to prove his theory: The Sphinx was solid rock. The head of the Sphinx was also damaged by Mameluke cannon fire during the Middle Ages, when the plain of Giza was used for military maneuvers.

Right, an inscribed tablet resting between the Sphinx's paws. It tells the story of a royal prince during the fifteenth century B.C. who returned from a hunting trip and fell asleep in the statue's shadow. In his dreams the sun god spoke to him and lamented, "I am sore depressed because of the desert on which I stand." The god then promised the prince a kingdom if he would only clear away the mounds of sand around the Sphinx's body. The prince obeyed and duly came to the throne as Thutmose IV.

One of the most important excavations conducted at Giza was that of the Valley Temple of Chephren, first studied by the Frenchman Auguste Mariette. This temple stands near the Sphinx at the Nile end of the causeway leading to Chephren's pyramid. It is thought that the pharaoh's mummy was embalmed here.

Left, the entrance to the Valley Temple. A symbolic false door, seen on the rear wall, was supposed to allow the ka spirit of the deceased to come and go freely. The surrounding carvings list food, clothing, and games that the ka would require in the afterlife. This information was provided for the guidance of the mortuary priests who remained in attendance after the pharaoh's funeral rites.

Right and below near right, the Hall of Columns in the Valley Temple. The uprights (13½ feet high) and their massive lintels are of red Aswan granite. Twenty-three life-size statues of Chephren once stood among the columns.

Below far right, the passageway which leads from the Hall of Columns to the causeway. This would have been the route followed by Chephren's funeral procession.

Of the Seven Wonders of the Ancient World, only the pyramids survive. Since Hellenistic times, when these monuments were already over two thousand years old, Giza had been a major tourist attraction. In ancient times, a visit here was thought to be the culmination of a superior education, just as in the eighteenth and nineteenth centuries the grand tour of Europe crowned the studies of the most well-bred British and Americans. Today Giza lies only a few miles from the expanding city of Cairo, whose residents may come here for an afternoon outing (above left). Tour guides (left, above, and right) are plentiful, and it is even possible to see Giza by hired camel.

The serenity of the Giza pyramids (following page) is still unmarred by their current popularity with world travelers. They remain, as always, impervious to time.

The Great Pyramids at Giza Egypt

"From the top of these monuments, forty centuries are watching you." With these words of exhortation, spoken on July 21, 1798, the twenty-nine-year-old Napoleon Bonaparte sent his troops into battle on the plain of Giza some eight miles from the Great Pyramids. Though the Battle of the Pyramids did not fulfill Napoleon's dream of turning Egypt into a permanent French colony, it did bring an abrupt end to Egypt's slumber under the reign of the Mamelukes, a Moslem military caste that had ruled the country for seven hundred years. In the wake of this brief campaign, Egypt was thrust into the center of international politics—where it remains to this day—and the ruins of its ancient kingdoms again became a magnet for European treasure hunters and scholars.

Napoleon confidently expected history to acclaim him, but he was quite prepared, in turn, to give history its due. Even as he was attempting to conquer the Nile Valley, 150 French scholars were busy measuring and drawing the Giza pyramids. And it was one of his officers, a young engineer, who discovered the famous Rosetta stone, a basalt slab bearing a text in three versions: Egyptian pictorial hieroglyphics, a scribe's phonetic form of the same ancient Demotic, and Greek. This stone was the key to hieroglyphic writing that transformed the study of ancient Egypt from speculation into science.

It is highly appropriate that modern Egyptology should owe so much, even if only accidently, to Napoleon's sense of his own imperial destiny. While others pondered the meaning of the pyramids, he dared to call on these monuments to witness his own triumphs and, in so doing, emulated the spirit of the pharaohs who created them.

Of all the creations of human civilization, the Pyramids of Giza are the most enigmatic. Numerous theories have sought to explain how and why such monuments were ever built. They appeared equally inexplicable 2,400 years ago when Herodotus, the "Father of History," recorded the story of his visit to Giza. In the second book of his *History,* the Greek chronicler described the plain's three major tombs, the pyramids of Cheops, Chephren, and Mycerinus. Like many observers after him, Herodotus could not resist the temptation to explain the structures, which were then already two millenniums old. He firmly believed that the pyramids were the work of tyrants, built by armies of slaves toiling under the lash. Cheops, said Herodotus, had put his own daughter into a brothel to finance his tomb; Chephren was "no better;" and Mycerinus, although equitable in his official conduct, had been guilty of rash impiety in trying to outwit an oracle who foretold his death. The *History* relates that the Great Pyramid of Cheops had been constructed over a ten-year period by 100,000 laborers and that they consumed over 1,500 silver talents' worth of leeks, onions, and radishes while working on the project. Herodotus also claimed that inside this pyramid the mummy of Cheops still lay on a stone island raised above an artificial lake of Nile water.

For today's Egyptologists, Herodotus'

Napoleon's scholars, who began their survey of Giza in 1798, were the forerunners of modern Egyptologists. Below, an engraving which shows them measuring the half-buried Sphinx.

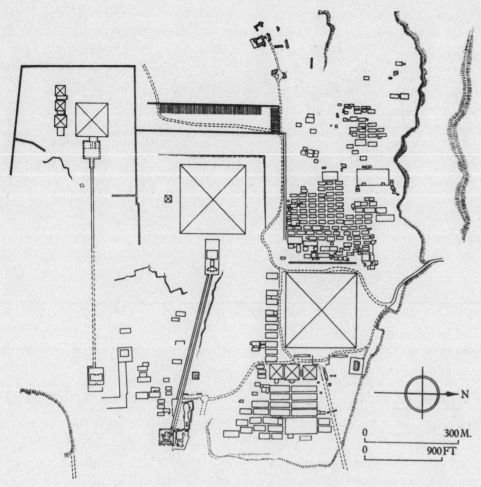

Above, a plan of Giza showing the tomb of Mycerinus on the left and the Great Pyramid of Cheops on the right. In the center is the Pyramid of Chephren with its restored mortuary complex.

Below, a cross section of the Pyramid of Mycerinus, showing its two entrances. The upper one leads to a dead end.

peaceful and prosperous. The persistent notion that the tombs were the product of forced labor has also been attacked by recent scholars, who suggest that the monuments may have served as a kind of public works project, employing farm laborers who would otherwise have starved during the three months every year when their fields lay inundated by the flood waters of the Nile. Even the romantic climax of Herodotus' story, the image of the mummy of Cheops resting in the middle of a secret subterranean lake, was a fabrication. No underground lake ever existed, and it is most unlikely that the body of Cheops was still inside his pyramid at the time of Herodotus' visit. The pyramids themselves may have proved durable, but ironically, they did not long succeed in protecting the remains of the pharaohs—much less for all eternity.

The monuments of Giza were certainly intended to be inviolable. The Great Pyramid of Cheops, the largest of the three, measures approximately 756 feet on a side and was originally 480 feet high, although some 30 feet have eroded from the summit. Of course, many modern skyscrapers are taller, but the Great Pyramid, with its three million cubic yards of stone, remains one of the most massive masonry structures ever built.

Its sole purpose was to provide a secure resting place for the pharaoh's mummy. The existence of additional abandoned burial chambers within the pyramid indicates that, even as it was being built, the designers changed their minds at least twice. Apparently, the original plan was to place the mummy in an underground chamber, which was to be reached by a descending corridor entered at the north face of the pyramid. A second chamber was later added above the first. Finally, a new ascending gallery, 28 feet high and 153 feet long, was opened off the original passage. This led to the actual burial vault. After the body had been laid in the vault, the ascending corridor was sealed by massive stone plugs. These were placed in the gallery at the time the pyramid was being built so that they could be later dropped into position.

account reveals more about the beliefs prevalent in Egypt at the time of his visit than it does about the creation of the pyramids. There is no evidence that Cheops and Chephren, who are also known as Khufu and Khafre, were inhumane and tyrannical. Their reigns, during the Fourth Dynasty of the Old Kingdom which began in about 2680 B.C., were on the whole

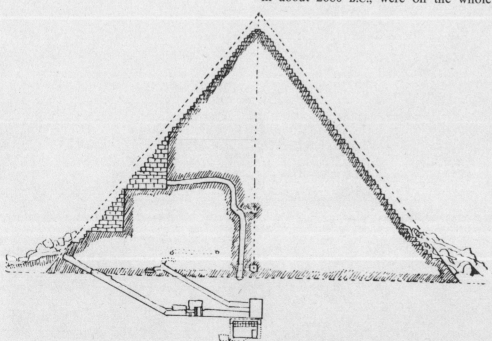

Despite these precautions, Cheops probably did not rest in peace for long. The fortunes in jewelry, gilded furniture, statuary, and other decorative objects that the pharaohs had entombed with them for their use in the next life were a great temptation to tomb robbers. Further, some historians have argued that Cheops was never interred in his tomb at all. They contend that the pharaoh may have died in an accident or that his remains may have lain without honorable burial, following a feud over the succession to the throne which is known to have occurred at the time of his death.

Whatever the truth of the matter, Cheops's burial chamber had most likely been plundered and resealed long before the visit of Herodotus in the fifth century B.C. It is recorded that the Great Pyramid was again opened in Roman times. And in the ninth century A.D., the Caliph Mamun, who was the son of Harun-al-Rashid, the legendary caliph of the *Arabian Nights*, had his workers bore a hole into the north face of the pyramid just below the old entrance to make sure that no treasure had been overlooked. Their battering apparently dislodged some large slabs from the ceiling of the ascending corridor, and the crashing of falling masonry led the men into the main gallery. The booty they sought was gone, but this did not stop the Arabs from circulating tales of phenomenal riches still hidden at Giza. The stories claimed that, in addition to jewels and gold, the tombs contained a magic antirust ointment and objects fashioned from a "flexible glass that does not break."

The first Europeans to penetrate the pyramids in modern times were surprised and disappointed to find that others had preceded them. No doubt the most brazen assault on a Giza pyramid was that led by Giovanni Battista Belzoni in 1818. A former circus strongman who turned to treasure hunting, sometimes on behalf of the British Museum and sometimes for personal profit, Belzoni was one of the most colorful characters of his age. He attacked the Pyramid of Chephren with a battering ram, and in the end, his muscle

Right, the entrance to the Great Pyramid of Cheops. Reinforced by limestone blocks, it is located 55 feet above ground level.

The smooth-sided pyramids, such as those of Cheops or Chephren (below right), were preceded by the so-called stepped pyramids like that of the Third Dynasty Pharaoh Zoser at Saqqarah (below).

combined with modern hydraulic equipment proved too much for even that gigantic monument. The stones gave way and the main burial chamber was opened—only to reveal that it, too, had been plundered long ago. Although it is true that Belzoni was sincerely interested in Egyptian culture and contributed much to the infant science of archaeology, his methods were enough to reduce later investigators to tears—and many of his finds

to smithereens. In one account of a dig near Thebes, Belzoni wrote, almost boastfully: "Every step I took, I crushed a mummy in some part or other."

Equally destructive were the investigations of the third and smallest pyramid, that of Mycerinus, who is also known as Menkaure. Belzoni had at least calculated the location of Chephren's burial chamber before beginning to pound away. Two Englishmen, Colonel Richard Howard-

Far left, a diorite statue of Chephren. Center, an ivory statuette of Cheops. Above, a slate statue group representing Mycerinus between the goddess Hathor and the goddess of the Jackal region. These statues of the builders of the Great Pyramids at Giza are now in the Cairo Museum.

Vyse and J. S. Perring, who attempted to enter the Pyramid of Mycerinus, simply dynamited a path to the interior. Luck was with them, at least for a time. A magnificent basalt sarcophagus containing human remains was found inside the tomb. Later research, however, showed that this mummy had been disturbed in antiquity and reassembled in about 600 B.C. during the Twenty-sixth Dynasty. Unfortunately, the sarcophagus was lost at sea while it was being shipped to England, and only the bones made their way safely to the vaults of the British Museum.

These early attempts to unlock the secrets of the pyramids by brute force produced little real knowledge about the monuments or their builders. Later investigators, turning their attention to the lesser structures in the mortuary complex, were far more successful. Through a strange twist of fate, the archaeologist primarily responsible for putting the Giza excavations on a scientific basis actually began his work by trying to confirm one of those mystical theories which are forever being propounded by amateur pyramid

buffs. In the second half of the nineteenth century, a Scottish astronomer and mathematician named Piazza Smyth had made a numerological analysis of the Great Pyramid's dimensions. He claimed that various measurements and ratios employed in the design could be used to foretell the future. One of Smyth's most fervent admirers was William Petrie, an English engineer with mystical inclinations. Impressed by the theory but skeptical of Smyth's data, Petrie sent his twenty-six-year-old son to Egypt to make a more precise survey.

Flinders Petrie proved to be no fly-by-night enthusiast. Arriving at Giza in 1880, he spent more than two years on a study which both disproved Smyth's calculations and constituted the first informed appreciation of the construction skills used 4,000 years ago. Petrie discovered that the sides of the Great Pyramid were oriented to true north, south, east, and west—so accurately that the maximum deviation was only half a degree. He also examined stone blocks weighing between two and a half and fifteen tons and found that they had been chiseled with extraordinary ac-

curacy: When fitted together, the joints averaged less than one-fiftieth of an inch in width.

Thanks to Petrie and his successors, we now know how this feat was accomplished. Herodotus' calculation of 100,000 laborers was a gross exaggeration; only about 4,000 workers—laboring without benefit of winches, pulleys, or wheels—toiled on the site of Cheops's pyramid in any one season. As the great limestone blocks, quarried at Tura on the east bank of the Nile, were brought across the river and unloaded, teams of about twenty men loaded them onto sleds and pulled them up the stone causeway to the foundations of the pyramid. The blocks of the inner core were laid in the stepped form visible today and then were surrounded with the limestone casing blocks. As successive courses were raised, Petrie hypothesized that ramps of dirt and rubble were built into the sides eventually reaching the summit and that these ramps were used to haul blocks to the upper levels. After the capstone was in place, the laborers, working downward, precisely cut and polished the limestone facing blocks.

Petrie's refutation did not signal the end of Smyth's theory, and variations of his numerological ideas reappear every few years. Yet the original reason for believing that there must be some paranormal solution to the riddle of the pyramids has long been discredited. Early archaeologists, like the Frenchman Auguste Mariette, believed that the pyramids were "mute;" that is, they contained no inscriptions. As long as the pyramids did not speak for themselves, there was room for speculation about hidden messages that might be incorporated into their architecture. It soon became apparent, however, that the absence of writings and interior decorations on the tombs of Cheops and Chephren was an exception to the rule. For whatever reasons, these monarchs had concentrated their resources on making their pyramids as large and well built as possible, but other excavations in the late nineteenth century showed that many of the relatives of these pharaohs had their own tombs decorated with fine bas-relief carvings.

Then in 1880 and 1881, a study of the Fifth and Sixth Dynasty burial ground at Saqqarah uncovered many examples of hieroglyphic inscriptions inside those pyramids. These so-called "Pyramid Texts," along with later papyrus manuscripts of the Egyptian "Book of the Dead," gave detailed answers to questions about the attitude of these ancient peoples toward mortality.

In some ways, the ancient Egyptians were more practical than latter-day students of their pyramids like Piazza Smyth and William Petrie. Their complicated burial practices did not reflect a fascination with mysticism so much as a satisfaction with life as it was and a profound faith in the logical order of the cosmos.

In contrast to Christianity, which sees our earthly existence as an imperfect interlude between a lost Eden and a vaguely

Above, a bas-relief from a mastaba chapel at Giza. It shows one of the sons of Cheops, Prince Khufu-Khaf, attended by his wife, receiving the funerary offerings presented to him. This is one of the earliest representations in relief showing two figures composed as a group.

Right, a limestone bust of Prince Ankhaf. The major achievement of the artists of the Fourth Dynasty, when the Great Pyramids at Giza were built, was the development of portrait sculpture. This delicately modeled bust is perhaps the finest such portrait to survive from the Old Kingdom.

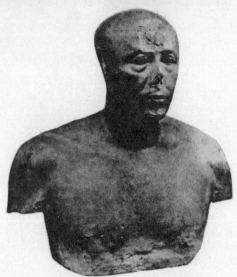

comprehended heaven, Egyptian religion taught that everything on earth was perfect, arranged precisely as the gods had wanted it and, therefore, not subject to change. Osiris, god of the underworld, had also been the legendary founder of the kingdom of Egypt, and his dominion was no less than a mirror of Egypt itself.

The logical extension of this view was the belief that the pharaoh, who was absolute ruler on earth, was a living incarnation of Osiris. Specifically, he was thought to represent Horus, the god's son, until after his death when he became reunited with Osiris.

Since the pharaoh's kingdom would continue eternally, all the accouterments of normal life were buried with him. In early times slaves were even interred in the tomb of the pharaoh as substitutes for his aristocratic aides. However, this grim practice soon gave way to the custom of providing *ushabti,* token figurines depicted in the act of performing various useful tasks. Even transportation was provided. According to the "Pyramid Texts," a properly outfitted pharaoh would need eight separate boats to carry him on his various celestial voyages. So far, burial pits for five such vessels have been found cut into the rock near the base of the Great Pyramid.

Lesser members of the ruling class could not afford to be so splendidly prepared for eternity. But their flat-topped tombs, or mastabas, which are clustered around the major pyramids of Giza, show that they too tried to insure that the afterlife would be as comfortable as possible. Those of lower rank had to anticipate that they might be called to serve Osiris, just as they had served the pharaoh in life. Surrounded by frescoes and carvings recalling highlights of their lives on earth, court functionaries and princes could be confident that their status would be recognized even after death.

By the early decades of the twentieth century, the exploration of mastabas and subsidiary temples was well under way. Many of these had also been thoroughly

Dynasty. Just when it seemed that archaeological work at Giza was becoming less interesting than it had once been, a member of Reisner's team made a discovery which was to rival anything that had been found there since the time of Napoleon.

The official photographer of Reisner's expedition was taking pictures in the vicinity of the Great Pyramid when one leg of his camera tripod suddenly sank into the ground. When it was drawn up, it was covered with white plaster—a clear indication of some subterranean construction. Further investigation led to a breathtaking find. There, buried under nine layers of

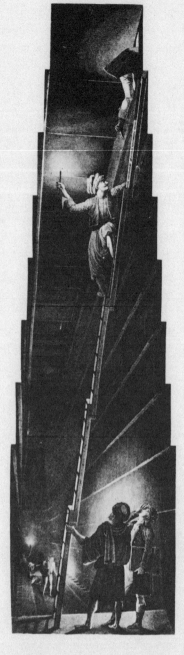

plundered, but some major surprises still lay buried under the drifting sands. The most successful archaeologist of this period was an American, Dr. George A. Reisner, who went to Egypt on behalf of the Boston Museum of Fine Arts. He became so immersed in the glories of this vanished civilization that he would sometimes regale visitors with anecdotes about "my people of the Pyramid Age."

Reisner's methodical excavation of two temples attached to the smaller Pyramid of Mycerinus uncovered a well-preserved trio of slate statues depicting the pharaoh in the company of two goddesses. These and other life-size sculptures discovered in Giza's mortuary temples have proved to be the chief artistic legacy of the Fourth

Tura limestone, was the funeral cache of Queen Hetepheres I, the mother of Cheops. Among the treasures in the tomb were alabaster vases, copper and gold utensils, and an exquisite bed and chair inlaid with gold—all unparalleled examples of Egyptian craftsmanship.

The archaeological team also found a jar containing the internal organs of Hetepheres and a wealth of lesser funeral appointments, including an alabaster manicure set and a case equipped with kohl and other cosmetics—priceless insights into the daily life of a queen who died some twenty-six centuries before the birth of Christ.

The triumph, however, had an anticlimactic end. After two years of painstaking

Mohammed Ali, viceroy of Egypt from 1805 to 1848, supported the work of French archaeologists in the Giza zone (above left) in the hopes that new evidence of Egypt's ancient splendor would contribute to the growth of nationalist feeling. Above, a nineteenth-century engraving showing the exploration of the gallery of the Great Pyramid.

Above right, a team of French archaeologists measuring a hand from a colossal stone statue. Right, a photograph taken in 1895, showing European tourists climbing the Great Pyramid.

effort to clear the tomb without damaging the fragile relics, the day came to open the queen's sarcophagus. The lid was slowly raised in the presence of an invited delegation of Egyptian officials—but the mummy was missing. This was, to say the least, a strange omission from a burial that almost certainly had not been disturbed since it was first sealed.

Reisner later theorized that Hetepheres had originally been buried away from Giza, near the pyramid of her husband Snefru in the old royal cemetery at Dashur. He hypothesized that Cheops, hearing that grave robbers were already at work in that area, may have decided to remove his mother's remains to a more secure site. This theory, however, did not explain why the sarcophagus had been carefully resealed, though empty. Reisner also suggested that there may have been a

palace conspiracy to keep Cheops from learning that his mother's corpse had, in fact, already been tampered with. If this is what happened, the conspirators were certainly successful. Hetepheres' absence from her own tomb was not noticed until 4,500 years after the event!

Mummies, the preserved physical remains of the dead, were central to Egyptian religious practice. Some of the best extant examples of the art of embalming, discovered at Luxor in Upper Egypt, still retain their skin and hair after 3,000 years. The royal mummies of the Giza necropolis did not fare as well, for the grandeur of the

burial ground made it a mecca for treasure hunters over the millenniums. But the studies of Auguste Mariette, George Reisner, and others have shed some light on how a pharaoh of the Fourth Dynasty was prepared for burial.

One of the best restored ruins at Giza is the Valley Temple of Chephren, located near the banks of the Nile at the beginning of the causeway which leads to his pyramid. This was probably the place where Chephren's body was actually embalmed, and it was certainly the scene of the various ritual purifications that would have preceded his funeral.

The preparation of a royal mummy was the work of several months. First, the brains were drawn through the nostrils

with a long metal instrument, and internal organs were removed through an incision in the left side of the body. The heart was left in place. By the Eighteenth Dynasty, this organ was believed to be weighed by Anubis, the god of death, on his scale of judgment. Once eviscerated, the corpse was packed in the mineral natron and dried for forty days. Later it was embalmed with oils and spices, including cassia, cinnamon, juniper essence, and onions. Any wounds were sealed with beeswax and the cheeks were dyed with henna to restore their color. Resins and gums were applied as preservatives, and the corpse was adorned with precious jewelry. The fingers and toes might even be covered with protective sheaths of beaten gold. Finally, all was wrapped in many layers of resin-treated linen. The brains and viscera, meanwhile, were carefully placed in a series of Canopic, or funeral, vessels which would accompany the embalmed corpse.

While the embalmers were at work, the household of the deceased would be in mourning. The hearth fires remained unlit, and the faces of the women and slaves were smeared with dust. A proper show of grief on the part of the survivors of the deceased was essential. The actual funeral arrangements, however, were far too important to be left to chance. Chephren, like any person of rank, would have made detailed provisions for his own embalmment and for employing mortuary priests and other functionaries. His death merely set in motion a process that had already been carefully planned.

The Egyptians realized that even the best-prepared mummy could not actually avail itself of the physical comforts provided for in its tomb. Their beliefs were based on the existence of the concepts of the *ka,* the *ba,* and the *akh.* The *ka* was a guardian spirit or double who guided individuals in life but was closely linked with their fortunes in the hereafter. The tomb was literally "the house of the *ka,*" and the luxuries of the burial cache were for the *ka*'s enjoyment. Thus, life-size statues of the deceased were often provided to act as substitute refuges for the *ka* in case

Right, the eastern façade of Chephren's Valley Temple as archaeologists believe it may have appeared originally. Between the two entrances is a stone kiosk containing a statue of the pharaoh.

the actual mummy should be damaged. Chephren was especially well equipped in this respect. No fewer than twenty-three statues of Nubian diorite stone were found in his Valley Temple, each thought to offer the *ka* a refuge corresponding to a different organ of the body.

Of the second spirit, the *ba,* less is known. It seems loosely identifiable as the soul, a life force which could leave the body after death and fly around freely. In paintings it is sometimes depicted as a winged figure with human features. Inscriptions and portraits left inside the burial chambers were intended to help the *ba* find its way back to the tomb at night.

The *akh* seems to have been that aspect of the noble dead which was transformed into eternal objects. The most noble were often conceived of as being transformed

Below, a nineteenth-century engraving of Chephren's pyramid, before the excavations of surrounding sites had begun.

into stars and thus joining in the changeless rhythm of the universe.

Only when Chephren's mummy was completely wrapped and encased in its coffin could his *ka* and *ba* assume their eternal roles. There are no extant accounts of the funeral of Chephren, but it was probably similar in many respects to the funerals which took place in later dynasties. Inside the Valley Temple, in the presence of assembled mourners, the temple priests probably conducted the all-important ceremony known as the "opening of the mouth." Touching the mouths of the mummy and its *ka* statues with ceremonial chisels and other tools prepared them to eat and speak in the afterlife. When at last Chephren was ready for the final leg of his "journey to the west," he was majestically transported through the enclosed corridor from the Valley Temple to his pyramid and symbolically toward the home of the god Osiris. In later dynasties,

the bier, drawn by a team of snow-white oxen, was accompanied by a large procession. The screams and moans of the pharaoh's grieving widows and children were augmented by wailing of professional mourners. In the burial chamber itself, a last feast of beer and bread was provided and a wreath of fresh flowers laid on the sarcophagus. But there was no tarrying in the tomb. After all the rites had been performed, the mourners retired hastily in a cloud of incense, leaving the pharaoh free to take up his identity as Osiris and to continue to enjoy the pleasures that were his by eternal right.

The road to the underworld was indeed a difficult one. The pharaoh who lived long enough to prepare adequately was fortunate. Short-lived pharaohs like Mycerinus had to depend on the benevolence of descendants who, after all, had their own tombs to prepare. And even important queens like Hetepheres risked having their graves despoiled almost before their funeral flowers had wilted and the cries of the mourners had ceased.

Nevertheless, the pharaohs of the Fourth Dynasty were certainly justified in believing that their kingdom would endure. In later centuries the absolute power of the pharaoh came to be shared with lesser princes and palace officials, and pyramid building itself became impossible. Of some eighty major pyramid tombs, those at Giza were the largest and most ambitious. But despite such changes, this Nile Valley civilization lasted for another two and a half millenniums, and the vast monuments of Giza continue to remind present-day Egyptians that their heritage is one of the oldest and richest on earth.

The Great Wall

People's Republic of China

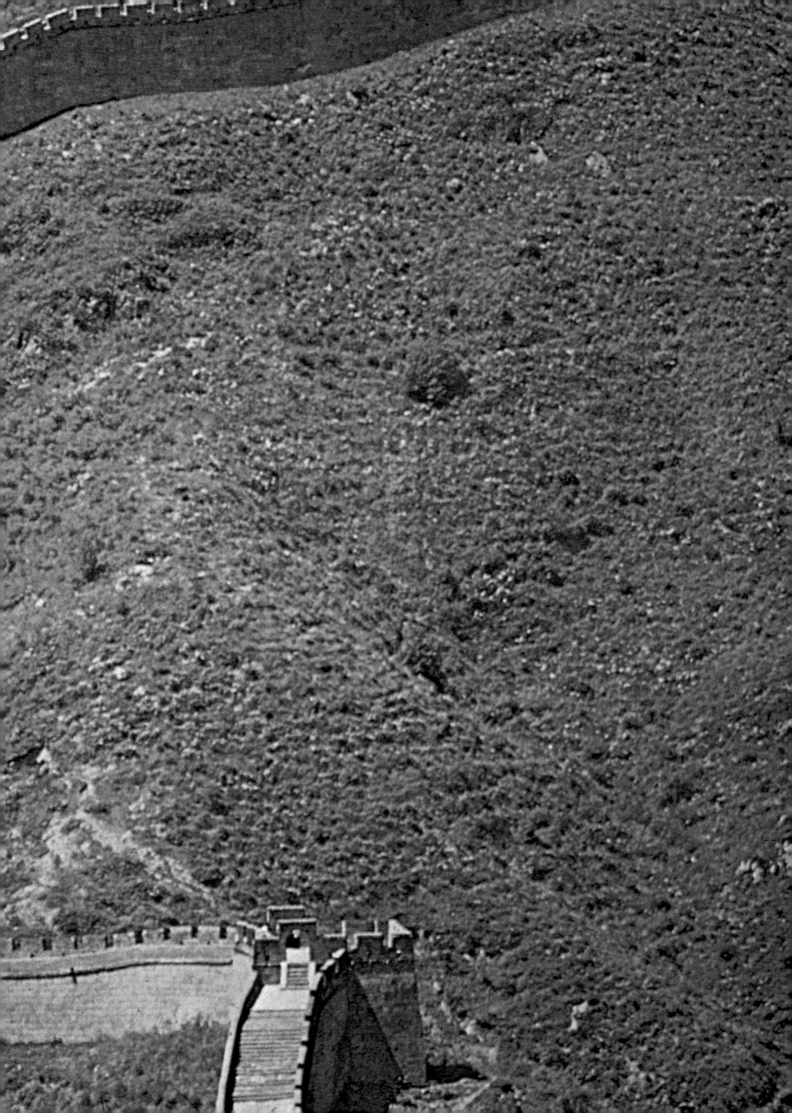

A sinuous stone ribbon, the Great Wall of China is said to be the only manmade construction which would be visible from the moon. The wall winds from the seacoast northeast of Tientsin west to the region north of Peking, cuts across the great bend of the Huang Ho (Yellow River) toward Lanchow, and finally proceeds along the southern border of the Gobi Desert. What remains of the main wall and its various ramifications measures between 1,500 and 1,800 miles, though the length of the original wall is thought to have exceeded 3,500 miles—a statistic that attests to the unmatched magnitude of the project. The wall was commissioned in 221 B.C. by Ch'in Shih Huang Ti, first emperor of a united China. Linking various tribal walls that were already in existence, the wall marked the border between agricultural China and the steppes to the north, while keeping nomads out and the Chinese in.

Preceding page and these pages, details of the eastern portion of the Great Wall of China just north of Peking.

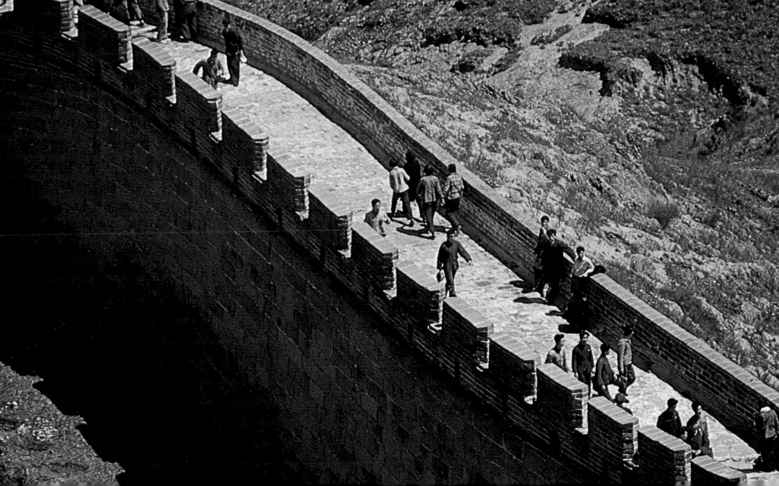

Left and right, details of the Great Wall, its roadway, and its fortifications. The wall was continually rebuilt, restored, and extended through the centuries. The last extensive reconstruction was during the Ming dynasty in the fifteenth and sixteenth centuries. The present government has restored parts of the wall and opened them to visitors.

After the expulsion of the Mongol dynasty in 1368, the wall was restored both for defensive and commercial reasons. Garrisons stationed in the fortifications were charged with colonizing and farming the formerly barren land on the northern border. Other fortresses were established where trade routes crossed the Great Wall, and numerous prosperous market cities grew up at these intersections.

The eastern sections of the Great Wall were built of stone. Two massive parallel foundation walls of dressed stone were laid up, and a fill of earth and rubble was tamped down between them with heavy tree trunks. A brick roadway was constructed over this for transporting troops and supplies. These masonry sections of the wall ranged from twenty to thirty feet in height. As a rule, the Chinese preferred to use rivers for travel and transport, but the Great Wall, once a smooth and highly efficient roadway, is a notable exception.

A recently restored section of the wall is open to tourists about twenty-five miles north of Peking. For centuries, foreign travelers, upon first seeing the wall, have marveled at its size. Viscount George Macartney, the emissary to China of King George III of England, remarked that it was "the most stupendous work of human hands." The present Chinese government has preserved the wall to commemorate the suffering of the Chinese people under past regimes. Like many of the world's spectacular monuments, the wall was built by forced labor at the cost of many lives.

The Great Wall People's Republic of China

Like one of the dragons of Chinese myth, the Great Wall curves sinuously across the length of China, from the seacoast at Shanhaikuan, northeast of Tientsin, to Chiayükuan along the southern border of the Gobi Desert. In some places, the wall follows the outline of the mountains as though it were a natural part of the rocky terrain. In others, it stands like a fortress against hills and sky, sweeping into valleys, disappearing, only to reappear on a distant peak. And then there are places where the wall is in ruins, a dim shadow of its own past.

The official length of the wall is thought to be about 1,500 miles, but this figure reflects only its distance from end to end as the crow flies. The actual circuitous course the wall covers is about 3,500 miles. This estimate includes the innumerable loops and bends, the multiple outer walls that mark successive campaigns of expansion into Mongolia, and extensions that leave the main wall at right angles. Its Chinese name—Wan Li Ch'ang Ch'eng—means Ten Thousand Li Long Wall. A *li* is equal to about one-third of a mile; but the word for ten thousand is used here figuratively, in the sense of "almost unimaginably long."

The Great Wall is without a doubt the longest defensive structure in the world. Shorter tribal walls are thought to have existed in China as early as the Shang dynasty, which lasted from the sixteenth to the eleventh century B.C. These and later walls protected one state from another as well as from nomadic tribes to the north. They were extended and unified into a single system by the Emperor Ch'in Shih Huang Ti, the brilliant if despotic ruler who united the Chinese states into one empire in 221 B.C. In the words of a Chinese historian, the young ruler swept across China "like a silkworm devouring a mulberry leaf."

Though the wall was to serve as a defensive border, defense was not the emperor's only purpose. To consolidate his power early in his reign, Shih Huang Ti had broken up the feudal estates of the former nobility, dispossessing the peasant serfs. As a result, he was left with a large, discontented population scavenging the countryside. Having already united China, and feeling no imminent threat from the nomads to the north, he had no immediate need for a large standing army. The construction of so vast a project as the Great Wall, however, would meet his combined goal of control over the potentially rebellious peasants within and of long-term security from the nomads without. Consequently, hundreds of thousands

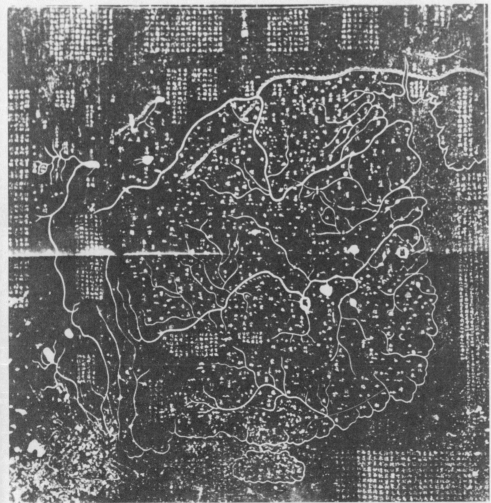

Left, an ancient Chinese map, dating from about 1100. Clearly visible in the upper part is the broken line that represents the route of the Great Wall. Above, engraving of a Chinese ruler from the book China Illustrated *by Kirker.*

Right, the trading post at Hormuz on the Persian Gulf, one of the ports at the western end of the legendary Silk Road between China and the West. Marco Polo passed through Hormuz on his way to and from China in the thirteenth century.

Left, an illustration depicting a typical fortified Chinese city gate. Below, a Mongol military encampment. The Mongols crossed the Great Wall from the north and finally conquered China in 1273.

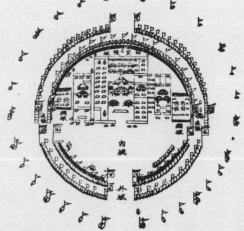

of young men—dissidents, prisoners of war, and state criminals—were conscripted to connect and strengthen the existing walls.

The project, under the direction of the military officer Meng T'ien, lasted from about 221 B.C. until Shih Huang Ti's death in 210 B.C. Once completed, the wall served a dual purpose. First, it restrained any Chinese farmers who might have succumbed to the temptations of the nomadic life of the northern steppes. The Chinese agrarian economy needed manpower if it hoped to prosper—China could not afford the loss of population that an open border would have permitted. At the same time, the wall was a geographic and cultural barrier, separating steppe from farm land. The traditionally xenophobic Chinese eventually came to look upon the Great Wall as the boundary of the civilized world, separating T'ien Hsia (All Under Heaven) from the darkness beyond.

Shih Huang Ti's original wall has been all but obliterated—in the east by frequent repairs made during later dynasties and in the west by time. It seems probable, though, that supply bases were built first and then the watchtowers, placed two bowshots apart so that archers stationed in each tower could defend the entire length of the wall. In addition, as many as 15,000 freestanding towers were built for additional protection on the north side of the wall.

The methods used in building the wall varied from district to district. Our knowledge of them derives from the extensive reconstructions carried out in the Ming period over 1,500 years after the wall was constructed, a program that apparently relied on the original techniques. In the rocky country to the east, the wall was made of brick and stone. Two massive parallel foundation walls of granite blocks served as a base which was in some places faced with brick. Between these two walls, the builders tamped down earth or clay using their feet or heavy tree trunks. A brick roadway was then laid between the two faces of the wall, allowing for the easy passage of supplies and troops.

Farther to the west, there was no clay for bricks and no stone for building a foundation. There was only loess, a yellow, silty soil excellent for agriculture but easily eroded. Since it was the only material available, an earthwork of loess was constructed and then covered where possible with a facing of stone or wood.

The populations of entire provinces are said to have been wrenched from their homes and forced into service on the wall. Thousands, perhaps millions, of Chinese laborers perished. According to legend, every stone in the Great Wall exacted the life of one worker. It is, therefore, grimly appropriate that the bodies of the conscripts were buried beneath the heavy stones of the wall, which earned its nickname as "the longest cemetery in the world."

Numerous legends surround the building of the Great Wall. Perhaps the best known is the tale of Meng Chiang Nu, whose husband, Fan San-lang, had been conscripted to work on the wall. One night while she slept, his spirit came to her bedside and told her that he had fallen and was buried in the wall. Chiang Nu anxiously set out to look for him: His fellow laborers confirmed her bleakest fear. But the gods took pity on the young widow. They caused a newly built section of the wall to collapse, exposing the bones of Fan San-lang. On her way home to bury her husband in his ancestral soil, Chiang Nu passed the traveling party of the Emperor Ch'in Shih Huang Ti. Struck by her beauty, the emperor requested that she join his household. But Chiang Nu was unwilling to live with the tyrant who had caused the death of her husband. She begged to have one hundred days to consider her answer. The emperor consented but insisted that she spend her time embroidering a gown for him.

When he saw the beauty of the gown she had made, the emperor demanded that Chiang Nu become his concubine. The widow pleaded for permission to first bury her husband on the seashore. No sooner had Fan San-lang's bones been buried than she leaped into the ocean, uniting her soul with that of her husband.

Under the Han and Wei dynasties that followed the Ch'in, work on the wall continued. In A.D. 423, the Wei emperor T'o-pa Ssu, second in the line of northern T'o-pa conquerors of China, added a new section to the Great Wall that was six hundred miles long. This extension was designed specifically as a barrier against the nomadic tribe called the Juan-juan, forebears of the later Tartar invaders. T'o-pa Ssu was thus the first, though not the last, emperor of China who, a foreign conqueror himself, took steps to keep other invaders out.

Though it can be argued that the wall was a better defense against sporadic raids than against outright invasion, armies from the north were able to penetrate the wall only when its defenders were demoralized by a weak government at home. During the fifth and sixth centuries, the Great Wall periodically lost its strategic importance. At this time, China was divided into many rival dynastic states, some ruled by tribes who had come down from the barbarian north. The wall was constantly being repaired, however, and for several years it successfully repulsed the invading Mongol horde led by Genghis Khan. But in 1273, his grandson—the legendary Kublai Khan—was finally able to break through. He soon established himself as the first foreign invader to control the whole Chinese empire.

The wall's function as a barrier became important again a century later, with the expulsion of the Mongols by the native Ming dynasty, which came to power in 1368. What exists today is, for the most part, the wall rebuilt by the Ming emperors on the ancient foundations. This reconstructed Great Wall stretched from the River Yalu in the east, on the border with Korea, to Chiayükuan in Kansu Province.

At the extreme northeastern end, the wall was nothing but an earthwork reinforced by densely planted willow trees.

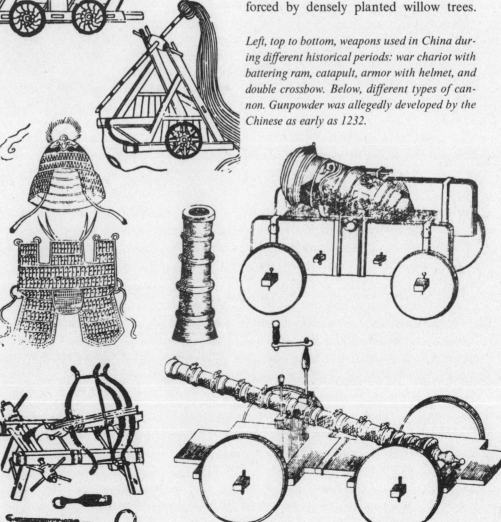

Left, top to bottom, weapons used in China during different historical periods: war chariot with battering ram, catapult, armor with helmet, and double crossbow. Below, different types of cannon. Gunpowder was allegedly developed by the Chinese as early as 1232.

Only very faint traces remain of this Willow Palisade. Westward from the Shanhaikuan Pass, on the border of the present provinces of Hopei and Liaoning, the wall was reconstructed of stone, much like the stone sections of the first wall. In the east the masonry wall was, on average, 15 to 25 feet high, 25 feet thick at the base, and 15 feet thick at the top. Five main gates were built in the wall at the major trade routes, each heavily fortified; other smaller gates permitted the flow of local traffic.

The main role of the wall was, of course, defensive, but it also functioned as an important line of communication in what is, for the most part, mountainous and rugged terrain. The Chinese were never great road builders, preferring to use rivers for transport. The Great Wall, a major artery, is a clear exception. The wall not only permitted troops to be rushed quickly wherever they were needed on the northern frontier but also functioned as a supply base, enabling the Chinese to establish colonies in the borderlands. These settlements failed, but only because the hostile climate in the north did not support traditional Chinese agriculture.

The Great Wall was a supply and trade route within China as well as a link to the outside world, permitting merchants to enter the country. For centuries, caravans came and went through the Jade Gate, the westernmost fortification of the wall, and

Soon after coming to power, the Chinese Communist government began to restore ancient monuments, including the Great Wall. Above, workers refurbishing the wall in 1950. Right, an aerial photograph of 1932 outlining the meandering route of the Great Wall.

crossed the desert west of China on the legendary Silk Road. The gate and the road were named after the commodities that were traditionally traded—the Chinese exported silk and imported jade.

Foreigners were allowed to pass through the gates of the Great Wall only in compliance with terms that suited the Chinese. At a time when European and Middle Eastern rulers were searching for far-flung markets and new lands to conquer, the Ming emperors stubbornly refused to admit that anything of value existed outside China. They kept up an elaborate charade whereby the merchants traveling the Silk Road were "ambassadors" bringing "tribute," in return for which they were offered "gifts." This myopic ritual persisted until the beginning of the nineteenth century.

Toward the end of the Ming dynasty in

1643, the Great Wall fell into such ruin that some sections disappeared entirely. Today the Communist government in China has, on the whole, been attentive to monuments that bear witness to the past, illustrating the creativity and sufferings of the Chinese people. So far, it has undertaken restoration work only on small stretches of the wall. Recent work projects have concentrated on the fortresses of Shanhaikuan at the eastern end and Chiayükuan, the traditional site of the Jade Gate, in the extreme west.

If the Great Wall has sometimes failed to act as a sufficient strategic barrier, it has nevertheless been a tremendously effective psychological boundary. A thin line indeed, now in many places altogether eroded, the wall has been a formative influence on the Chinese people both physically and symbolically for two thousand years.

Jaipur Observatory

India

Preceding page, a panoramic view of Jaipur Observatory. Built around 1734, this was the second of five such groups of instruments erected by Maharajah Jai Singh to follow the movements of the stars and predict celestial events. The maharajah was also interested in improving the accuracy of astronomical tables then used in the East, but his stone instruments failed to give precise readings—not so much because of their unorthodox construction but because their enormous size tended to magnify imprecisions. The instruments, with their graceful supporting arms and beautifully curved surfaces, are as much sculptural as functional and strikingly anticipate modern Functionalist architecture. In fact, the observatory achieved the greatest recognition in the 1950s, when Abstract Expressionism—then at its height—strongly influenced the development of modern architecture.

Top left, the Samrat Yantra, or "supreme instrument," that dominates the observatory. The
Samrat Yantra is a prodigiously large equinoc-
tial sundial "for finding time, declination, and
hour angle of the heavenly bodies." Adjacent to
the Samrat Yantra is the Rasi Valaya Yantra
(remaining photos on these pages), which is a
collection of twelve ecliptic instruments, one for
each sign of the zodiac. When the particular sign
is on the horizon, the instrument indicates the
sun's latitude and longitude.

Left, the Nari Valaya Yantra. An immense solar clock, it consists of a masonry cylinder about ten feet in diameter oriented along a north-south axis. Its two faces are parallel to the plane of the equator and form dials which are graduated in hours and minutes.

The finely calibrated scales of Jai Singh's great sundials were capable of far more precise measurements than would be possible on smaller instruments—far more precise, unfortunately, than the shadows that they were intended to measure. Near right and center right, the Rasi Valaya Yantra. Far right, the Samrat Yantra.

The Ram Yantra (below) is one of a pair of instruments also used to calculate the position of the sun. Radial lines on the floor indicate the azimuth, or horizontal position; calibrated degrees on the walls and floor record the sun's height. The Ram Yantra at Jaipur is a copy of one Jai Singh had built in Delhi.

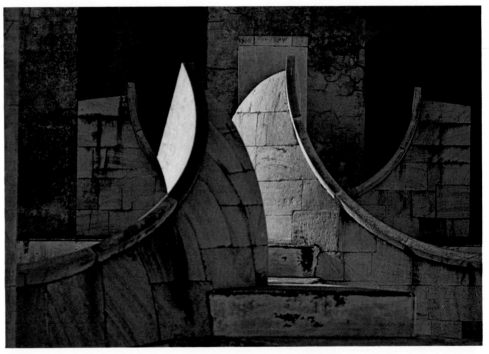

The gnomons, or triangular masonry shafts, of the Samrat Yantras (above) cast shadows from which readings can be taken. The great Samrat Yantra (right) has a gnomon ninety feet high, with its hypotenuse parallel to the north-south axis of the earth. It is, however, so big that its shadow is too blurred to be read accurately. Left, one of the circular marble quadrants of the Samrat Yantra which is graduated in degrees, minutes, and seconds. The gnomons of the smaller Rasi Valaya Yantras (below) are oriented toward the pole of the ecliptic when particular signs of the zodiac are on the horizon.

Much of the special beauty of the Observatory at Jaipur results from the precise play of light and shadow. Circular forms, such as the ones on these pages, are placed in an aesthetic relationship to the angular structures, creating the simple, sculptural harmony sought by Le Corbusier and other twentieth-century architects. Above and above right, the Jai Prakas, a large, marble hemisphere for determining the position of celestial bodies. Near right, the Unnatamsa Yantra, a brass circle just over seventeen feet in diameter. Center right, two disc-shaped astrolabes, each seven feet in diameter. One is made from sixty sheets of iron riveted together; the other is brass. Far right, the finely graduated surface of the brass astrolabe. Following page, the Observatory at Jaipur seen from the royal palace.

Jaipur Observatory India

In many Eastern societies, names have great symbolic value. Parents give their children names signifying particular virtues, in the hope that they will grow up to embody those qualities. When the future Maharajah Jai Singh II of Jaipur in Mogul India was born in 1686, his parents named him Jai, meaning "victory." The maharajah certainly lived up to his name, if not in war, at least in the consolidation of his power. He ascended the throne when he was only thirteen and not only retained but also strengthened his principality. Yet if today he is remembered at all, it is not for his accomplishments as a ruler, but for his one great passion—astronomy. This

enthusiasm led Jai Singh to build the series of open-air observatories, whose masonry instruments are some of the most fascinating structures throughout the Indian subcontinent.

In 1699, Jai Singh became the ruler of Amber, now known as the region of Jaipur—a principality in the province of Rajputana in northwest India. The inhabitants of Rajputana (today the state of Rajasthan) believed themselves to be the descendants of the *ksatriya,* the ancient Hindu caste of warriors, and preserved a long tradition of courage and loyalty founded upon the heroic ideals of the ancient Hindu epics. Even the Mogul emperors who governed them treated the rulers of Amber with especial respect.

At the time Jai Singh commenced his rule, the Mogul empire, which governed in India from 1526 to 1761, was beginning to decline. Under the weak and inexperienced Mohammed Shah (1719–1748), its territory was subject to numerous invasions, while dynastic convulsions sapped its strength from within.

In this time of intrigue and warfare, Jai Singh proved so skillful as a statesman

that he earned the reputation of the Machiavelli of India. In 1719, he was appointed governor of the province of Agra and, soon after, of Malwa. Under his able control, peace was maintained throughout his lands. He built secure trading compounds throughout the countryside, and in 1728, he founded Jaipur—the city of Jai, or the city of victory—as a new capital in the principality of Amber. The previous capital, the small fortress-city of Amber, was completely deserted.

The new city was designed as a magnificent monument to princely sovereignty, a capital city worthy of the illustrious maharajah. Set amid rugged mountains in northern Rajasthan, it is surrounded by a crenelated rose-pink wall, twenty feet high, which has earned it the name of the Rose City. Eight splendid portals lead into the city. The buildings within are painted in the same glowing pink, often decorated with white curling motifs.

Like many eighteenth-century cities, Jaipur is a monument to rationality. Jai Singh was personally interested in city planning, and before beginning work, he

Above, the fortified city of Amber, which was the capital of the Kachwaha Rajputs until Jai Singh founded the nearby city of Jaipur in 1728.

Right, one of Jai Singh's stone instruments, compared with the type of metal instruments more commonly used during the same period.

Left, the Hawa Mahal, or Palace of the Winds, where the wives of the Rajput maharajah lived. The name derives from the decorative screens on the windows, which allowed breezes to enter while preserving the privacy of the women within.

Above, a miniature depicting a dignitary from the court of Rajputana.

Left, a fanciful miniature—a popular form of Rajput art—showing a stylized fight between trained elephants.

consulted with architects and astronomers and studied plans of the most modern European cities. The fruit of his efforts was one of the first Indian cities to follow the grid pattern so common to modern Western cities. In Jaipur, houses were built in traditional Indian style, with corners of finely dressed stone and balconies supported by pointed Oriental arches.

In the midst of this remarkable city stood the vast palace of the maharajah, a small town in itself. Covering one-seventh of the land in the city, the palace was protected by pink walls and towers and contained a series of large courtyards surrounded by official and domestic quarters. It was in one of these courtyards that Jai Singh built an observatory equipped with extraordinary astronomical instruments made of stone, plaster, brass, and iron. The uniqueness of these monumental instruments—sculptures on an architectural scale—is emphasized by their distinctly Eastern setting.

The Jaipur Observatory was neither the first nor the last constructed by this dedicated stargazer, although it is the best preserved and the most beautiful. In 1724, Jai Singh had erected his first observatory in Delhi. Next, he built Jaipur in 1734. And before the end of his reign in 1743, he built three others, at Benares, Ujjain, and Mathura. The last of these was vandalized for its valuable stone and has disappeared. But the other four remain, fascinating testimonies to the maharajah's consuming passion for astronomy.

For Jai Singh and his contemporaries, astronomy was a discipline quite unlike the science we know today. His observatories were used more for astrological purposes than for purely scientific ones. Accurate forecasts of the dates for religious and royal events required a precise foreknowledge of the interrelated movements of the stars and planets, which in turn required precise tables of astronomical data. Jai Singh owned an extensive library containing the work of European astron-

omers, such as Flamsteed and La Hire, as well as that of Euclid, Ptolemy, and the Moslem Ulugh Beg. Eager to improve upon the calculations he found in their tables, he undertook the task of preparing more accurate computations. He sent researchers abroad for further information, invited several European priests interested in astronomy to Jaipur, and, in time, built his own observatories. Ironically, his calculations turned out to be of little value.

Jai Singh published his observations and calculations in a work which he dedicated to the Mogul of India. It is therefore known as the *Zigh-i Mohammed Shahi*, the *Tables of Shah Mohammed*. In the preface to the book, the maharajah (referring to himself, with scientific objectivity, in the third person) outlined his motives as follows:

He found that the calculation of the position of the stars as shown in the tables in current use...diverges notably in many cases from what is established by observation, and that in particular at the appearance of the new moon, the computation does not agree with observation. As a great number of solemn festivals, both imperial and religious, are connected with the results of these calculations, while many analogous variations are found at the time of the rising and setting of the planets and the seasons of eclipses of the sun and moon, he represented these tables to His Majesty the Emperor....

The emperor had authorized the maharajah to "rectify the disagreement." To do so, Jai Singh continued:

...not finding the equipment then in use at all to his liking, he constructed in Dar al-Khilafat Shah Jahanabad (Delhi) instruments which he had himself invented, such as the Jai Prakas, the Ram Yantra, and the Samrat Yantra, which has a semidiameter of eighteen cubits, and on which one minute corresponds to a grain and a half of barley. He had these constructed in stone and lime, of perfect stability....

Jai Singh's instruments, which were actually enlarged and modified versions of existing ones, were his attempt to solve the problems which he considered had been the stumbling block to accurate astronomical readings in the past. He claimed that most of the instruments in use in the seventeenth and early eighteenth centuries were made of brass and were adversely affected by changes in temperature, wear of the parts, and vibrations in the supporting framework. In addition, these instruments were generally very small, making it difficult to make measurements with the requisite precision.

Jai Singh believed that these problems could be overcome if instruments could be made large enough to have more finely calibrated reading scales. He therefore increased the size of his instruments so that they could be graduated in seconds as well as the customary degrees and minutes. He also constructed his instruments on a massive scale, using durable, rigidly fixed ma-

In Jai Singh's India, the study of the heavens was astrological as well as astronomical, seeking a meaningful connection between man and the cosmos. Left, below left and right, and bottom left, astrological diagrams. By encouraging spiritual concentration, they were thought to bring men closer to the things of heaven.

Right and below right, signs of the zodiac. The rulers of Mogul India customarily consulted their horoscopes before making even the most mundane decisions.

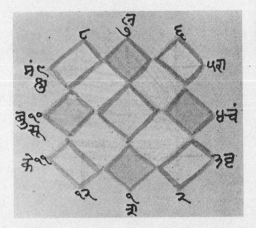

terials that were impervious to climatic changes and vibration.

Not surprisingly, the advantages of the maharajah's innovations were offset by a number of severe limitations. To begin with, his instruments were much more costly to build than smaller models. Even apart from this, construction was laborious and slow because each piece of stone had to be fitted and placed perfectly to insure accuracy. Furthermore, as the instruments were fixed and could not be rotated to follow the paths of the celestial bodies, observation was limited to a single part of the sky.

Jai Singh partially overcame this drawback by building some of his instruments in sets of twelve—one for each astrological sign. But his massive instruments had one fundamental and irremediable flaw. Though tremendous effort had been invested in their conception and construction, they were designed for viewing the heavens with the naked eye, a technique that had been rendered obsolete more than a century earlier when Galileo developed the telescope in 1609. At the time Jai Singh was constructing his prized observatories, contemporary Europeans were working with far superior instruments, and their observations were both more precise and more extensive than those possible at Jaipur.

The maharajah, however, may have been less interested in being up to date than in creating an observatory that would correctly express the active relationship between his earthly kingdom and the workings of the cosmos. Thus, his instruments had a spiritual dimension in addition to their purely astronomical function. The great sundial of the Samrat Yantra and the round stone faces of the Nari Valaya Yantra were designed to demonstrate this cosmic relationship as well as to make scientific measurements. In this sense, the instruments would have been, in Jai Singh's eyes, ultimately superior to any simple telescope, no matter how scientifically advanced.

Jaipur is the best preserved of Jai Singh's five astronomical observatories. Here the profound, curiously modern beauty of his huge stone instruments— some reaching ninety feet in height—is most evident. Like enormous abstract sculptures, these carefully shaped, ascetically smoothed *yantras* (instruments) are devoid of ornamentation. Their mysterious appeal stems from their simplicity and the harmonious juxtaposition of rounded and straight lines. One has only to sit within the gigantic circular stone platform of the Samrat Yantra, just as Jai Singh himself did every day to direct observations over two hundred years ago, to feel the almost surrealistic power of these huge instruments.

It is uncanny that these great, stargazing monoliths should so clearly prefigure the functional architecture of the twentieth century—especially since Jai Singh never indicated that they should be regarded as monuments or as the embodiments of a particular theory of architecture. He simply stated that he wanted to build accurate instruments. Nevertheless, the great modern Functionalist architect Le Corbusier would have been delighted with the instruments at Jaipur, for they exemplify all that he believed good architecture should be: "the correct, skillful, and magnificent play of volumes composed in light."

Yet the Jaipur Observatory is more than a fortuitous architectural by-product. It also expresses the desires of a people to understand their place in the cosmos. Jai Singh's calculations may have proved insignificant to modern astronomers, but the poetry of his instruments survives in an unworldly conjunction of art and science.

Left, a sixteenth-century Islamic astrolabe, used for determining the height of stars on the horizon. It was used in conjunction with disks which represent a different area of the sky.

The Nubian Temples

Egypt

*"Nothing like it has ever been made before."
This boastful pronouncement, which Rameses II
had carved on his cliff temples at Abu Simbel,
became doubly true in the 1960s when the monuments were totally reconstructed in the course
of a massive international rescue operation. Because they were threatened by the rising waters
of an artificial lake created by the Aswan High
Dam, the temples were raised to a safe location
over 100 feet above the old valley floor.*

*Preceding page, a dramatic aerial view of the
new site, showing the artificially landscaped
cliffs. Concrete structures behind the cliffs support the temples. Seen from eye level (above left
and left), the temples appear very much as they
did in their original setting.*

*Rameses II built the Queen's Temple (right and
above right) to honor his favorite wife, Nefertari.
Flanking the entrance of the temple are six
standing figures, four of Rameses himself and
two of Nefertari, who wears a diaphanous gown
and a headdress bearing the cow's horns and
solar disc—emblems associated with the goddesses Hathor and Isis. Decorations on the interior of the temple again identify the queen with
Hathor, the feminine deity of love and happi-
ness. The smaller figures grouped around the
legs of Rameses and Nefertari represent a few of
the pharaoh's children. Rameses not only had
over 150 offspring by various wives but also
married three of his own daughters.*

Left, one of the four seated colossi that guard the Temple of Rameses II. When the explorer John Lewis Burkhardt reached Abu Simbel in 1813, only the head and upper torso of this one statue were visible. Archaeologists have dated the rising level of the dunes from the graffiti carved by ancient travelers on the legs and chest of the figure. A relief carving from the temple (above left) shows Rameses driving his chariot at the Battle of Kadesh. Above right, a detail of a fanciful, fat-bodied insect. Below, Nubian captives, bound at the neck, carved on the south wall of the temple. Right, a small statue of Nefertari, who wears a crown decorated with sacred cobras.

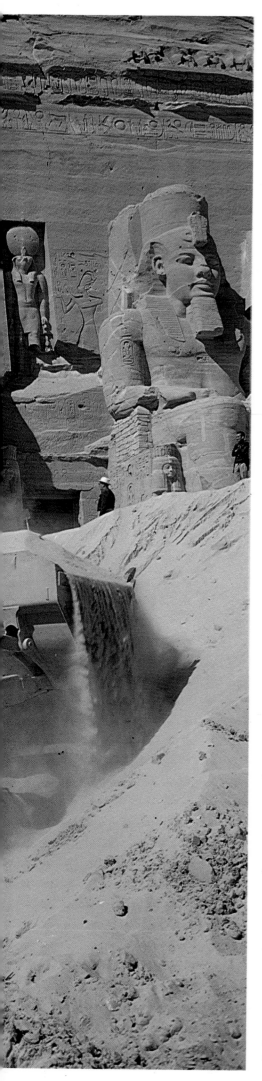

Preceding page, the façade of the Temple of Rameses as it appears today. Carved directly from the sandstone cliff, the monolithic portraits have been vulnerable to natural faults in the rock, such as the one which shattered the head and torso of the second figure in ancient times. Some modern repair work can be seen on the leg of the figure at the far right. Re-Horakhte, the falcon-headed sun deity, stands in a niche above the temple door, flanked by carvings of Rameses in the act of worship. Ranged around the colossi's feet are various queens, princes, and princesses. In addition to Nefertari, who appears several times, one of these small figures is Mut-Tuy, who was Rameses' mother and also one of his official wives.

UNESCO's project for rescuing the Abu Simbel temples was an engineering feat far more difficult than their original construction. The site (far left below), with the hole where Rameses'

temple once stood, is already partly flooded. The temporary dike, which protected the temples from water damage prior to the project's completion, and the access roads built for heavy equipment are also inundated (far left above). The colossi (near left), so laboriously dug free by earlier archaeologists, are once again buried to protect them during removal of the upper portions of the façade. Above, the seated figures on their new site.

Cutting the soft sandstone of the temples into twenty-ton blocks and reassembling the pieces accurately called for an unprecedented standard of precision. During dismantling, a sheet metal tunnel (bottom left) was used to maintain access to the temple interiors. Workers (top left) delicately reposition one of the blocks, while others toil at the foot of the reconstructed cliff, which will simulate the original setting. A foreman (center left) examines the condition of a newly reconstructed hand.

Work progresses under the watchful gaze of the three massive heads of Rameses (above). With their false beards (emblematic of the god-king Osiris) temporarily removed, the faces assume an uncharacteristically gentle expression. UNESCO experts took pains to see that no accident befell these heads, which had survived thirty-three centuries of neglect. The finely chiseled eye (right) shows the porosity of the stone.

As the rescue of Abu Simbel drew to a close in late 1967, international teams of archaeologists and construction experts turned their attention to other important Nubian monuments. The most important of these was the temple complex of Philae, a center of the cult of the goddess Isis, which flourished during the Ptolemaic and Roman eras. The little island of Philae (preceding page) was once renowned as the "pearl of Egypt." Since the construction of the first Aswan Dam in 1898, it has been flooded for all but three months of each year. This photo, taken from the new site projected for the temples on a higher neighboring island, shows Philae surrounded by a 66-foot-high cofferdam that was erected in 1972 to hold back the waters for the duration of the project.

Top left, drums from the temple columns standing disassembled and ready for the move.

Center left and right, the main Temple of Isis before it was dismantled. Dark bands around the base of the temple mark previous high-water levels. Relief carvings on the temple's front pylons represent the Pharaoh Ptolemy Neos Dionysos, his arm raised in the act of vanquishing his enemies. This motif was standard in Egyptian art from about 3000 B.C. The smaller door, visible to the left of the main entrance, leads to the mammisi, a sanctuary where every year Isis was thought to give birth anew to her son, Horus. The free-standing archway is the Gate of Philadelphius, added by Ptolemy II as part of a ceremonial passageway.

Bottom left, decorations on the smaller second pylons of the Temple of Isis, depicting Isis and Horus, the falcon-headed god. A flagpole was once mounted in the deep groove between the figures.

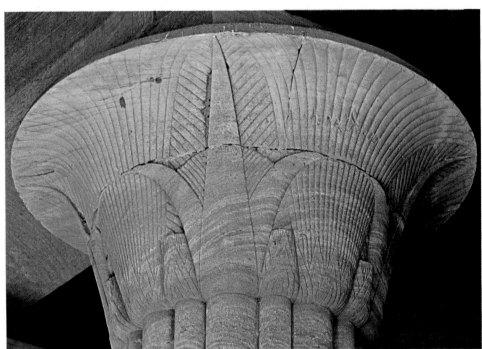

Facing page, the Kiosk of Trajan, which held the sacred boat of Isis. Every ten days the priests ferried an effigy of the goddess to the island of Bigah for a ritual visit to her husband Osiris.

The ornate columns of Philae represent the culmination of three thousand years of religious iconography. Above left, a column from the mammisi sanctuary, crowned by a stylized head of the goddess Hathor and a small model of the naos, or sacred room, of the sanctuary. Imaginative floral motifs (top right) decorate the capitals of pillars along the length of the dromos, or avenue (left), which leads to the main entrance of the temple. Above, a capital from the Kiosk of Trajan. It takes the traditional form of a bundle of reeds, topped by an abstract floral design.

Isis, the "Lady of Philae," was one of the most important deities of the Egyptian pantheon. Over the centuries she became associated with a number of other goddesses and was depicted in a variety of guises. Far left above, the most familiar representation of Isis. She wears the solar disc and cow's horns, also connected with Hathor, the patroness of the Queen's Temple at Abu Simbel. The columns (far left below) of the eastern colonnade show the goddess in the lion-headed form of Isis-Meht. The fame of Isis was international and her cult continued to thrive long after the Roman occupation of Nubia. Thus, Philae became one of the last traditional Egyptian temples in active use. Although the temple was not even begun until the fourth century B.C., its colonnades (left and above) exemplify building methods that are considerably older. The roofing of the western colonnade, with slabs of stone merely laid across the gap between inner and outer walls, is a typical example of the ancient architectural solutions employed here.

Ptolemy Neos Dionysos, a pharaoh of the Greek dynasty which ruled Egypt before it finally fell to Rome, had himself portrayed at Philae as a traditional Egyptian pharaoh. Above, a relief showing him worshiping Isis and her son. He is pictured below making offerings to a group of seated gods.

Near right and far right above, details of reliefs showing the most popular forms of Isis. Chisel marks on the figure of the pharaoh (far right center) are evidence of an attempt by sixth-century Christians to destroy these pagan idols. Far right below, images of the gods which have been cut through with a Coptic cross.

Unlike Philae, which attracted pilgrims for six centuries, the temples of Abu Simbel (following page) seem as if they have always stood in lonely desolation. Although there is no evidence that the Nubians ever actively worshiped these colossi, the gods that Rameses II helped establish in Nubia eventually became deeply entrenched in that region.

The Nubian Temples
Egypt

"Ruins, monuments, magnificent buildings, cataracts, deserts, haunts of wild beasts, or men (as wild) as they. . . ." These were the wonders unveiled in an eighteenth-century narrative of a 750-mile journey up the Nile from Cairo to Philae, near the First Cataract of the river in Upper Egypt. When its Dutch author, Frederick Norden, published the account of his travels, it was an immediate success—scarcely surprising, since Norden had penetrated a land that his contemporaries regarded as the most romantic and mysterious on earth. Cairo and the Great Pyramids of Giza were exotic in

themselves, but the upper reaches of the Nile were a true *terra incognita.* Norden's descriptions of Philae were particularly intriguing to his readers. This small island, five miles beyond the village of Aswan, was the gateway to the land of Nubia—the ancient kingdom of Cush and the fabled source of the pharaohs' gold.

Eighteenth- and nineteenth-century Europeans were not the first to find romance in the name Nubia. For the ancient Egyptians, the region was a half-tamed frontier and the source of much of their kingdom's mineral wealth. As early as 2600 B.C., the Pharaoh Cheops established a diorite quarry on the Nile, 150 miles south of Philae near Abu Simbel. Ivory, brought by caravan from central Africa, was traded at the Elephantine market of Aswan, and over the centuries, Nubian granite, amethysts, and above all, gold were the riches that enhanced the lives of the pharaohs. The Egyptians also regarded the Nubian Desert as the home of the life-giving Nile. The true source of that great river was unknown to the civilization that was so entirely dependent upon it.

Nubian loyalty to Egypt fluctuated according to the fortunes of its distant rulers. Although early dynasties had fortified the Nile well upriver from the First Cataract, there were frequent rebellions, interspersed with periods of calm when strong pharaohs were able to exercise firmer control over the desert tribes. When Nubia was finally integrated into Egypt, the Nile kingdom had already begun its slow process of disintegration, and this once-reluctant colony became the last defender of Egyptian civilization. In the eighth century B.C., the king of Cush actually marched north, assumed the pharaoh's crown, and attempted to reimpose traditional values on the decadent Egyptians. But this Cushite dynasty soon collapsed, and Egypt fell prey to a series of foreign conquerors, including the Persians and the Ptolemies.

The Romans eventually reached the First Cataract and established Nubia as the southernmost outpost of their vast empire. But the Nubians were slow to give up their ancient traditions and customs. While Lower Egypt gradually became

Rameses II (above) leads a successful campaign against the rebellious tribes of Nubia. The small size of the enemy soldiers dramatizes their inferiority to the pharaoh.

The statue (above center) of one of Rameses' many wives is probably Isisnofret, who was second in importance only to Nefertari (shown at right with Rameses).

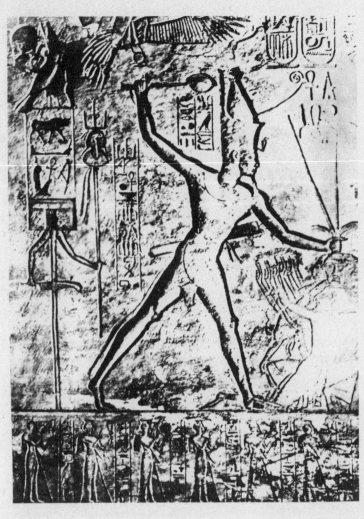

part of the Hellenistic and Christian worlds, Osiris and Isis, the first family of the Egyptian pantheon, were making their last stand on their island strongholds of Philae and Bigah in the region of the First Cataract.

In 1737, when Frederick Norden reached Philae, only a few ruined temples remained as evidence of the tenacious loyalty of the ancient Nubians to their adopted culture. The political situation was anarchic, and for a European to travel south of the First Cataract was virtually unthinkable. Even in the 1770s, James Bruce, the intrepid Scotsman who explored the upper reaches of the Blue Nile, one of the river's two major tributaries, was forced to bypass the Nubian Desert and reach Ethiopia by way of the Red Sea. Only after 1811, when the new ruler of Egypt, Mohammed Ali, sent his son Sheik Ibrahim to govern the upper Nile, did any order emerge.

At this time, the Swiss traveler John Lewis Burkhardt was visiting the area on behalf of the British African Association. Burkhardt took full advantage of the new opportunity to push southward. He spoke fluent Arabic and was also a perceptive observer and careful note taker, qualities rarely found in the explorers of those days. Like Norden, Burkhardt was fascinated by the temples of the Philae region. But he was even more excited by rumors of a still more magnificent and ancient temple, reputed to be located on the banks of the Nile some 150 miles upstream.

Burkhardt finally reached this place, known in Arabic as Ipsambul, or Abu Simbel, in March 1813. But his moment of discovery was initially disappointing. Expecting the colossal edifice of popular reports, Burkhardt instead found only the much smaller Queen's Temple, guarded by six standing statues, four of the Pharaoh Rameses II and two of his favorite queen, Nefertari. This monument, 92 feet long and 39 feet high, was no small find, but it was not enough to fulfill Burkhardt's high expectations.

Later, however, as Burkhardt was ex-

ploring the surrounding cliffs, he stumbled on a tantalizing sight. Protruding from the drifted sands was a stone head of massive proportions, and the tops of two similar heads were discernible nearby. Burkhardt realized that, if the stories he had heard were true and these heads belonged to seated figures, they would rank among the most imposing monuments of the whole Nile Valley. He predicted that, if the sand could be cleared away, a huge temple would be discovered.

Others were inspired by Burkhardt's find. Four years later, Giovanni Battista Belzoni, a former circus performer and treasure hunter, managed to enter the great temple by tunneling through the sand dunes. In lieu of the portable treasures he was searching for, he encountered only a hellish heat and some incomprehensible inscriptions. Later archaeologists, who deciphered the writings that Belzoni had found meaningless, were far more impressed. Periodic excavations and restorations brought to light more and more of the temples' buried secrets, revealing that Abu Simbel was one of the finest temples built by the audacious Egyptian ruler, Rameses II.

Rameses II is remembered as the epitome of pharaohs. Yet his dynasty, the Nineteenth, was founded by a commoner and came to power only as the result of a series of tragedies which began in the reign of Akhenaton, a ruler who was Rameses II's antithesis in every respect. Akhenaton was a brilliant and innovative thinker who cared more for philosophy than for warfare or administration. He denounced polytheism and instituted a new monotheistic faith. He also moved his capital downstream from Thebes to the city of Amarna, where he and his beloved queen Nefertiti lived in simple domesticity—setting a standard for the rest of the court. Even the official art of this period reflects Akhenaton's radical ideas. The stylized portraits favored by former pharaohs were replaced by paintings and statues which copied and even exaggerated Akhenaton's protruding belly and large chin. Stiff formal poses were abandoned in favor of affectionate domestic scenes,

Above, a nineteenth-century print of the façade of the Temple of Rameses. Below, a print of the Great Hall of Pillars inside the temple. The pillars are weight-bearing statues of the ruler in the guise of Osiris. The ceiling is embellished with flying vultures.

often showing members of the royal family hugging and kissing.

Conservative Egypt, however, was no place for a poet-king. Akhenaton aroused the enmity of both the priests and the generals, and his reign collapsed in a series of personal misfortunes. No one knows exactly what happened to Akhenaton, but it appears that even Nefertiti deserted him, and his daughter's husband, the pharoah's chosen heir, died young. Akhenaton's second son-in-law, Tutankhamen, inherited a very troubled kingdom and also died when he was less than twenty years old.

Tutankhamen's childless widow, Ankhesenamen, made a dramatic attempt to improve Egypt's deteriorating military position by arranging to marry a Hittite prince. But the bridegroom-to-be was murdered on his way to Egypt, probably by the queen's enemies. Akhenaton's line thus died out, and the throne of Egypt was occupied by a series of viziers and generals, the last of whom was the grandfather of Rameses II.

Although Rameses II was only about eighteen years old when he became coregent of Egypt in 1304 B.C., he quickly set out to build a legend that would identify him and his family with the divine power

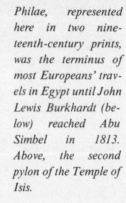

Philae, represented here in two nine-teenth-century prints, was the terminus of most Europeans' travels in Egypt until John Lewis Burkhardt (below) reached Abu Simbel in 1813. Above, the second pylon of the Temple of Isis.

of the pharaoh. His great personal victory over the Hittites at the Battle of Kadesh, fought in his fifth year, became the keystone of his reputation. His scribes and temple artists recorded this exploit in such expressive detail that early Egyptologists at first mistook them for epic fiction, calling them the *Poem of Pentaur*. This poem relates how Rameses completed an unprecedented march of more than four hundred miles into Hittite territory in less than a month. There, while personally leading the farthest advances of his corps, he was tricked into an ambush by two Bedouins claiming to be enemy deserters. Rameses was then said to have held off the entire Hittite force almost single-handedly for several hours until Egyptian reinforcements finally arrived. Kadesh was thus not only a glorious triumph but also proof that the pharaoh was personally favored by the gods.

Although the image of Rameses holding back an entire army aroused some skepticism, this version of the battle stood for some three thousand years, until the discovery of a contemporary Hittite account which relates that Rameses actually lost the battle. Either way, Rameses' exploitation of the campaign demonstrated a genius for propaganda. By the end of his long reign, the Nile kingdom was carpeted with temples, statues, stele, and other monuments glorifying his name. Thebes, Egypt's traditional administrative capital, was thoroughly remodeled, existing temples were enlarged, and a giant funerary temple, known today as the Ramesseum, was constructed.

For a ruler determined to make his symbolic presence felt along the whole length of the Nile, the desolate Nubian cliffs must have presented an irresistible challenge. A remote village, known in ancient times as Meha and today as Abu Simbel, came to Rameses attention, probably because of its chapel dedicated to the god Horus, son of Osiris. Rameses transformed this minor shrine into two impressive temples.

The smaller of the two, and the one described by John Burkhardt, is a shrine to Nefertari, Rameses' favorite among his many wives. Its interior antechamber and entrance hall are filled with statues and carvings of the cow-headed goddess Hathor, often portrayed as receiving the tributes of Rameses and Nefertari. The temple's elaborate decorations and the beautiful, thinly clad statues of Nefertari on its façade are evidence of Rameses' affection for his principal wife. But as Hathor was associated with Isis, the mythological first queen of Egypt, the statues also symbolized the political strength of Rameses' queen.

This message was echoed in Rameses' own temple, which was almost entirely hidden behind the four 60-foot-high seated portrait figures of the pharaoh. Its entrance hall was lined with eight enormous statues depicting the pharaoh as Osiris. And bas-reliefs and sculptures inside the antechamber and sanctuary proper showed Rameses worshiping a variety of gods, including the sun deities Amon-Re and Re-Horakhte (or Re-as Horus), as well as himself. Inscriptions warned that this temple was the work of

Above, a sketch made for the UNESCO rescue mission. It identifies major cracks in the façade which posed difficulties during the dismantling process.

These two drawings (right) from a rejected Italian proposal envisioned enclosing the temples in huge concrete boxes heavily reinforced with steel and then raising them intact with 650 synchronized jacks. Permanent concrete foundations were to be placed underneath the temples until they could be raised above the level of the lake.

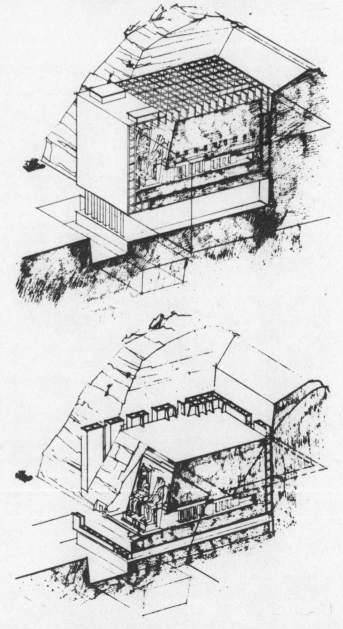

"the fearless one who no longer permits the existence of the land of the Ethiopians" and recounted the highlights of the Battle of Kadesh. In these writings, the pharaoh, faced with the Hittite forces, calls on Amon-Re with a plea that is a mixture of pious formulas and royal hubris:

> I filled thy holy house with my prisoners. I built for thee a temple of millions of years. . . . Let thou order an evil fate to befall him who attacks thy excellent decrees, and a good fate to him whom thou accountest just. . . .

Modern students of Egyptian history often find it easier to empathize with the gentle individualist Akhenaton than with Rameses II, whose passion for building approached megalomania and who tirelessly promoted his own legend. Experts disagree on the artistic merits of Rameses' temples. Some feel that in his pursuit of sheer size he sacrificed the grace achieved by previous dynasties, while others have been deeply moved by the majestic calm of the colossi at Abu Simbel.

Amon-Re himself must have been greatly pleased by his "temple of millions of years," for he and the other ancient gods continued to dwell in Nubia long after they were no longer worshiped in Egypt proper. After Rameses II, the power of the pharaohs waned and few major monuments were constructed along the Nile. Yet the history of Nubia's most vital temple complex—that found at Philae—was just beginning.

The island sanctuary of Philae first came to prominence in the fourth century B.C., when the pharaohs of the Thirtieth Dynasty, ancient Egypt's last indigenous ruling family, began constructing a major temple to Isis there. Always one of the most popular Egyptian goddesses, Isis was believed to have rescued the body of her husband Osiris after he was murdered by another jealous god, thus making his eventual resurrection possible. In this way Osiris also became the prototypical mummy. As a paragon of feminine virtue and womanly mysteries, Isis later became a cult figure throughout the Classical world. The Greek Ptolemies, who adopted the Egyptian religion when they came to power after 330 B.C., paid particular attention to Isis, the "Lady of Philae." And under this Thirty-first and last dynasty, the island's temple complex was further

Left, the Temple of Rameses when the rescue operation began in 1964.

A schematic drawing (right) of the UNESCO salvage plan shows the ramp of sand used to protect the lower parts of the colossi while the upper parts were being disassembled. It also shows the temples in their projected new sites.

expanded. Ptolemy VI Philometor added a small shrine to Hathor, the patron goddess of the Queen's Temple at Abu Simbel. Another Ptolemy, Neos Dionysos, had himself commemorated on the walls of the main temple, in the act of sacrificing to Isis and vanquishing her enemies. These reliefs are similar in style and theme to the narrative carvings which appear in Rameses' temples, although they lack the latter's imposing self-confidence. They also had a comparable purpose: to assure the Egyptian people, and perhaps themselves, that the Ptolemies were the legitimate heirs to the divine power of the ancient pharaohs.

The Romans, who entered Egypt after the defeat of Antony and Cleopatra by Augustus, felt less need to justify their presence to Amon-Re, Hathor, or anyone else. But they, too, revered Isis, and during the first and second centuries B.C., Roman governors in Nubia had the Philae temples enlarged yet again. It was at this time that the cult of Isis finally reached its apogee.

Soon after, Egypt began to be converted from pagan beliefs to Christianity. But the rituals of Isis continued to be observed in Nubia for several more centuries. Every ten days, the island priests placed an effigy of the goddess in her sacred boat and ferried her to the nearby island of Bigah for a ceremonial visit to the legendary grave of Osiris. Until the fourth century, the priests kept a flock of sacred falcons, and new inscriptions were added to the temple walls as late as A.D. 473. Finally, in the year A.D. 550, the Emperor Justinian ordered the shrine closed, and the island briefly became the site of a Christian church. In 641, Lower Egypt was conquered by the Arabs: The "Lady of Philae" far to the south was forgotten and, for the most part, so was Nubia.

After Napoleon Bonaparte's invasion of Egypt in 1798 and the defeat of the Mamelukes, Egypt again looked to the southern desert as a source of potential wealth. It soon became apparent, however, that Nubia's most valuable resource was no longer gold or semiprecious stones, but water. The Greek historian Herodotus had called Egypt the "gift of the Nile." But what the ancients had been happy to accept as a gift, modern man was determined to take for himself and harness. British engineers realized that, if the flow of the Nile could be controlled at the First

Above left, one of the massive heads of Rameses being lifted into place.

Above, the official inauguration of the rebuilt temples of Abu Simbel on September 22, 1968. It was attended by representatives of the forty nations who participated in the project.

Cataract, irrigation down river could be improved and the disastrous impact of drought years eased. In 1898, a dam was erected at Aswan, and in consequence, many of Nubia's most beautiful temples were inundated for most of each year. Scholars and art lovers mourned, but most of the world was content to accept the temples' slow destruction as a sacrifice to progress.

By the 1950s, the old dam was no longer considered sufficient, and a new, much larger structure, capable of supplying hydroelectric power to the developing nation, was proposed. This Aswan High Dam was itself a miracle of engineering, containing seventeen times as much building material as the Great Pyramid of Cheops. But it would exact a staggering price. Nubia's island temples, including Philae, would be totally submerged, and even Abu Simbel, far upstream, would be flooded by the rising waters.

Egypt's Minister of Education and Culture brought the impending tragedy to the attention of the United Nations. The Nubian Desert soon swarmed with cultural and scientific expeditions. Abu Simbel, in particular, was x-rayed, photographed, surveyed and studied from every conceivable angle with a view to recording its glories, soon to be lost for posterity.

In the end, the world rose to the challenge, and many plans were developed for

actually preserving the temples themselves. One Italian proposal suggested raising the Temple of Rameses intact with a gigantic contraption composed of 650 hydraulic jacks. The less grandiose solution eventually adopted by UNESCO was still immensely complex. The Abu Simbel temples were cut into huge blocks weighing approximately twenty tons each. These were raised to a nearby plateau above the projected water line and reassembled on a site landscaped to resemble the temples' original setting in the valley cliffs. By the time this operation was completed in 1967, it had cost over $36 million.

UNESCO also turned its attention to saving other Nile temples, especially the monuments to Isis on Philae. Here, too, the most dramatic rescue proposal was never carried out. Originally, engineers had hoped to save the entire island by enclosing the immediate area with a series of subsidiary dams. The United States allocated $6 million for this project in 1960, but the scheme was judged impractical. UNESCO decided that the Philae temples should simply be moved to a neighboring island of higher elevation.

In 1972, Dutch engineers constructed a temporary protective dike around the temple complex, and teams of specialists began an exhaustive survey of the monuments and identification of their elements for subsequent reassembly. The technical

problems encountered at Philae were, in their own way, more complex than those posed by the Abu Simbel project. Instead of merely cutting a group of monolithic statues into stone blocks, the workers had to dismantle the temples so that the weight-bearing elements would continue to perform their function after the rebuilding. Work at Philae has proceeded smoothly, and by 1980, the Temple of Isis will be in its new setting and ready to welcome visitors year-round for the first time since the turn of the century.

Today's Egyptians are extremely proud of Abu Simbel and Philae and frequently invite foreign visitors to contemplate the ironies of Nubia's history. This region, until recently considered remote and backward, has not only become the site of some of the most sophisticated exercises in international cooperation ever attempted, but has also managed to preserve more of its past than many nations with a longer consciousness of their national heritage.

The Sugar Loaf
of Rio de Janeiro

Brazil

The beauty of Rio de Janeiro, with its long white beaches, rain forests, and emerald lagoons, is seen most commandingly from the conical peak of Sugar Loaf Mountain (preceding page). Even at 1,300 feet above sea level, the informal sprawl of the city suggests the healthy exuberance that characterizes Rio to the world.

Sugar Loaf, or Pão de Açúcar as it is called in Portuguese, stands at the entrance to the Bay of Guanabara. This twenty-mile-long inlet of the south Atlantic was first discovered by Europeans in the sixteenth century, but few vestiges of the colonial period have survived Rio's post-World War II economic boom. Although the new prosperity has brought luxury hotels and crowds of tourists, Rio is still best known for a centuries-old celebration, an exultant dance of life popularly known as Carnival. In a last fling before the austerities of Lent, the entire city is swept up in a pageant of frenzied dance, music, parades, masquerade balls, and riotous street festivities.

The summit of Sugar Loaf can be reached both by day and night via funiculars, or cable cars. The peak was first scaled in 1912 by a team of Austrians, and the original funicular came into service later that year. One cable car runs between the Vermelha Beach and an adjacent mountain, the Morro da Urca. A second takes passengers to the peak, which commands a sweeping view of Copacabana Beach (center right) as well as Corcovado, Rio's tallest mountain (above).

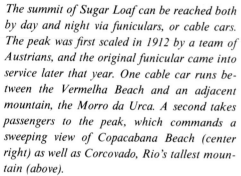

In many ways, Rio is as much beach as cosmopolitan city. The city's renowned beaches—Botafogo and Flamengo on the bay and Leme, Leblon, and Ipanema (immediately below) on the Atlantic—attract thousands of tourists each year, but they are also integral to the daily life of the Cariocans themselves, both socially and economically. Vendors throng the beaches, crying out "Sanduiche!", and beach-side cafés sell caipirinha—clear brandy, mashed sugar, and limes—to locals and tourists alike.

Right, Copacabana Beach, which stretches for three and a half miles. This section of the city is the most densely populated in Brazil, with 25,000 inhabitants per square mile.

The Sugar Loaf of Rio de Janeiro Brazil

The sea dominates life in Rio. It was from the sea that the first Portuguese conquerors and colonists arrived, and through the sea that Brazil reached out to other lands. Sea meets land on the elegant, curving beaches of Rio's South Zone: Copacabana, Ipanema, Leblon. These districts, a solid phalanx of high-rise hotels and apartments, face directly onto the south Atlantic. The beaches are the pride and delight of their inhabitants, their very raison d'être.

Like a backdrop, a coastal range of steep mountains juts upward, walling off the new South Zone from its older and larger northern counterpart. Rising some 2,300 feet out of this scrub-covered range is the mountain known as Corcovado, the Hunchback. On its summit stands a huge statue of Christ, with arms outstretched over this Catholic city.

The nearby summit of Sugar Loaf (the Pão de Açúcar), rising nearly 1,300 feet above the sea, is a natural beacon on the western edge of the Bay of Guanabara. The name of the mountain derives from its conical shape, which resembles an eighteenth-century sugar loaf. It is also an allusion to the primary colonial crop of Brazil. Sugar Loaf is to Rio what the Acropolis is to Athens or the Eiffel Tower is to Paris: a symbol instantly recognizable throughout the world.

At Sugar Loaf the coastal range abruptly parts, permitting the Atlantic waters to sweep into the Bay of Guanabara, on whose shore sits the North Zone of Rio. If the beaches of the South Zone represent pleasure, then the bay symbolizes prosperity. Well-protected from storms and easily defended, the bay placed Rio well ahead of rival towns.

Over the last century, Rio's North Zone has spread inland from its western shore. Remarkable construction feats have accompanied this advance. As early as 1892, tunnels were bored through the coastal range to give access to the Atlantic beaches. Hills and ridges were decapitated, and the soil was carried off to transform swamps into residential areas. The more important mountains were opened to visitors by cable cars and roads that abound in switchbacks and hairpin turns.

The mountain soil, however, is easily eroded. Heavy rains trigger landslides in Rio much as they do in southern California. Nevertheless, the lack of land suitable for building has pushed the *favelas* (shantytowns) up the mountain sides—up toward the chic restaurants and the eagle's nests of the very rich.

The population of Brazil and especially of Rio is growing at a spectacular pace. There were just over 30 million Brazilians in 1920, 52 million in 1950, and 115 million in 1978. One of every two South Americans is Brazilian; and one of every two Brazilians is under twenty-five. Rio's population numbered 1.1 million in 1920, 2.4 million in 1950, and 6 million in 1977. There are predictions of a population of 18 million in Rio's greater metropolitan area by the year 2000.

Brazil's population explosion has created a host of problems, in addition to housing shortages and automobile-clogged streets. Brazil has an acute short-

Above, Pedro Alvaro Cabral, the Portuguese navigator who is credited with the discovery of Brazil. He landed at the present site of Rio in 1500.

Right, the fleet of the Dutch admiral Oliver Van Noort at anchor in the Bay of Guanabara in about 1599.

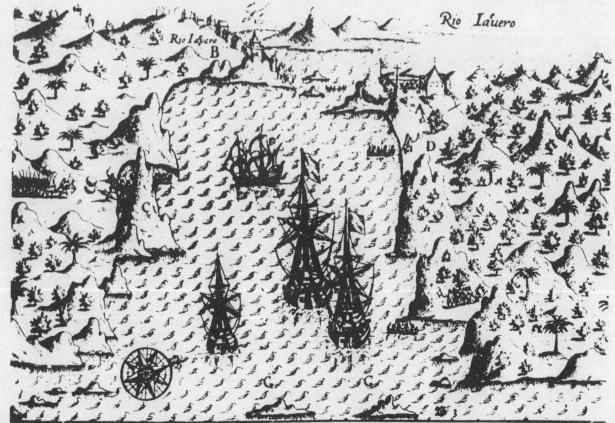

Above right, Dom John, the regent of Portugal (later King John VI) and his son Pedro (above left). Accompanied by a sizable retinue (left), they settled in Rio in 1808 to escape the French invasion of Portugal. In 1822, Pedro led Brazil to independence and became its emperor.

Brazil. Brazil is now the fifth largest country in the world, whose 3.3 million square miles of land nearly equal those of the continental United States. Its hugeness made it barely governable in an age of horses, ox-drawn carts, and sailing ships. Settlement was confined to a narrow coastal strip and centered upon a few port cities. Rio became the most important of these when it became the capital in 1763.

By then the diamond and gold rush of the inland province of Minas Gerais had brought boom times to Rio. Prospectors arrived en masse; roads and inns were built for the mule trains; and a financial community developed. Despite Rio's emerging importance, it remained in many ways a cultural backwater. The Portuguese, concerned about movements toward Brazilian independence, forbade newspapers, education, and foreign trade in the town, and its inhabitants were kept ignorant of European events. However, when the prince regent of Portugal, Crown Prince John, took up residence in Rio in 1808, he was so appalled at the ignorance of his colonists that he devoted the thirteen years of his stay to modernizing the city.

John opened the port to foreign commerce and permitted foreigners to open shops in the city. A chamber of commerce, a national bank, and a chemical laboratory were established along with theaters, museums, and schools. Rio was transformed, albeit temporarily, from a center of government on the rim of an impene-

Above, an old print of Botafogo Beach, with Sugar Loaf rising in the mists beyond.

age of efficient service industries. Every resident of Rio can tell stories about sudden electrical breakdowns (passengers trapped in stalled elevators are not uncommon) and the fizzing sound that sometimes replaces water when faucets are turned on. Moreover, the scarcity of telephone equipment retards new installations by many months, and influential Cariocans (natives of Rio) frequently employ impressive ingenuity along with payoffs to have their needs satisfied quickly. Letters are best mailed only at post offices, as the ones entrusted to the stylish Art Nouveau mailboxes of central Rio sometimes molder there for months.

All these difficulties are lamented, but not necessarily regarded as serious. For Rio has the good-natured, casual spirit of a tropical resort. Cold weather is unknown; the rains are intense but short; clothing is informal, often minimal; and the beaches are open to all. Here, the venturesome go courting; the athletic enjoy volleyball, paddle ball, and soccer; and the poor escape Rio's hot spells.

This sensual, hedonistic Rio exists alongside another Rio—of power and dynamism, of economics and politics. It resides in the modern office buildings of the central districts, though its roots reach back to the Portuguese era. Rio was founded in 1565 and soon ranked as the major administrative center for southern

Top, a Portuguese family of the colonial era, accompanied by a black nursemaid. The Palace Square (bottom), which with its tiled roofs, stuccoed walls, and iron balconies could just as well be in Portugal.

trable continent to the capital of a substantial empire. The lesson was not lost on those Brazilians who had begun thinking of independence. A year after the departure of Prince John in 1822, Brazil declared its independence from Portugal.

There was a growing foreign colony, primarily of diplomats, English businessmen, and once the Napoleonic Wars ended, French artists and architects. These newcomers built homes, sometimes on a palatial scale. The most desirable location was atop the mosquito-free northern and western hills. Much was done to drain the wetlands near the shore, a first step in the Cariocan's long struggle with the environment, shaping and molding it to meet urban needs. The process still continues, without too much concern for ecology or aesthetics. Such concerns are alien to the dynamic and aggressive tendencies of the Brazilians.

These qualities were certainly very much present in the Rio of the late nineteenth century. With the advent of the railroad, steamship, and telegraph, Rio was able to tap the agricultural wealth of distant provinces, to ship it abroad, and to communicate with banks and stock exchanges across the globe. The coffee boom also had a tremendous effect on the country. Huge fortunes were made—and squandered—overnight. A crop of coffee millionaires appeared, whose conspicuous consumption simultaneously benefited, impressed, and irritated the Cariocans.

Rio, once primarily a city of bureaucrats, now served more and more as a funnel through which raw materials poured out to the Northern Hemisphere and through which arrived the colonists, capital, technology, and goods that Brazil needed for development. Like Shanghai and Singapore, Calcutta and Cape Town, Rio had become a great interchange where contrasting cultures and lifestyles converged and joined.

One of these influences was African, first introduced into the country through slavery. The slave trade, declining by stages, was entirely ended by 1850, but slavery survived in Brazil until 1888. African influences are still present throughout Brazil, particularly in religion, popular culture, and the wide variety of skin colors visible in any crowd. Rio's favelas are heavily populated by Afro-Brazilians, for whom social and economic advancement remains largely limited to the areas of sports and entertainment.

Though both Rio's commerce and population were booming by 1900, the city itself was, in many respects, deficient. Streets were unpaved; the sewage and water systems were grossly inadequate; and the seasonal recurrence of smallpox, yellow fever, and bubonic plague led the wealthy to migrate to the mountains for the summer months. A vigorous public health program that began in 1903 quickly brought results, while the city was dramatically rebuilt over the same period.

The mode was French: that of Baron Haussmann's improvements to the Paris of Napoleon III (1852–1870). In the French capital, sewers and water mains were laid under beautiful boulevards and elegant streets. Similarly, the unplanned colonial city of Rio was transformed into broad, monumental boulevards, squares, and Classical government buildings. The methods employed at Rio were frequently ruthless. Buildings were demolished en masse, sometimes in night attacks, to out-

The installation of Rio's first funicular (above) in 1912 stirred the imagination of Rio's citizens. Ladies and gentlemen of a more formal era (top right) look down on Rio from the Corcovado (Hunchback). Center right, an eighteenth-century aqueduct, Rio's answer to a perennial problem: a scarcity of water. Sedan chairs (bottom right) were once popular among the fashionable residents. Here, a noble woman emerges from her discreetly curtained chair.

flank those owners who refused to vacate their property.

The purpose of these building campaigns was perhaps as much psychological as physical. They were intended to impress the world with Brazil's triumph over backwardness and, above all, to create an emotional focal point for Brazilians themselves. Centrifugal tendencies had always been powerful in Brazil, with its disparate regions, ethnic groups, and opposing classes. A majestic capital might counterbalance these dangers, by impressing the population with the tangible power of a state that purported to represent the national interest as no single group could. In the early 1960s, the government was transferred to Brasília, but to many, Rio still represents the soul of Brazil.

In any event, the seriousness of government is treated ironically by most Cariocans, who go their own way, mixing excitability with hedonism. For many, the highlight of the year is Carnival, the four days before Ash Wednesday. Carnival is a Portuguese import, dating back to the mid-seventeenth century, but its vigorous, exuberant, and sensual character derives entirely from the African and Indian strains in Brazilian life.

During Carnival, egalitarianism reigns and the people of the favelas come into their own. After skimping and saving all year, they spend lavishly on fantastic, often voluptuous, costumes. Their individual virtuosity is channeled by the hundreds of Escolas de Samba, highly organized clubs whose thousands of members spend months practicing for the huge processions down the main boulevards.

Fantasy and exhibitionism end by dawn on Ash Wednesday. But the mood doesn't quite end: Every Cariocan can think ahead to the same time, next year.

Empire State Building

New York City

As it rose during the Depression, the Empire State Building seemed to symbolize America's strength and faith in the future. Constructed in the months immediately following the great stock market crash of 1929, it has dominated the New York skyline for almost fifty years (preceding page and left) and was for four decades the tallest building in the world. Over forty-seven million tourists have visited the landmark since its opening in May 1931.

The tower is 102 stories tall and is surmounted by a 222-foot spire. Its ziggurat shape is partly the result of the 1916 zoning regulations that required buildings to be set back from the street above a certain level to let in light and air. Many of New York's older buildings conform almost diagrammatically to this specification, which was in effect until 1960. Although only one-fourth of the office space in the Empire State Building was leased during its first year, today it is always almost fully occupied.

John J. Raskob of General Motors Corporation, who organized the construction project along with Pierre S. Du Pont, had the pylon on top of the building designed as a mooring mast for dirigibles, though it was never actually used for this purpose. Instead, it was adapted and lengthened in 1950 for use as a television transmitter. With the addition of an FM antenna in 1965, the spire became one of the largest transmitting stations in the world.

Right, a dizzying view from the base of the Empire State Building; below, a few hundred of its 6,500 windows.

Most of the façade is covered with Indiana limestone and granite. Vertical strips of a glossy, stainless steel alloy achieve a streamlined emphasis, characteristic of the Art Deco style of the 1930s. The same alloy frames each of the windows. The architectural firm of Shreve, Lamb, and Harmon submitted seventeen designs to the Empire State Corporation, which was formed only a few weeks before the contractors began demolition of the old Waldorf-Astoria Hotel on the corner of Thirty-fourth Street and Fifth Avenue. The chosen plan, the sixteenth, made maximum use of advances in steel framing, which allowed for an unusually flexible internal layout.

Above, the understated canopy at the entrance to one of the world's most famous buildings. For many years, the Empire State Building had no street address, but recently, under pressure from the postal authorities, it has been listed as 350 Fifth Avenue. Located in the commercial center of Manhattan, it lies midway between Pennsylvania and Grand Central stations.

Right, a tour guide standing in front of one of New York city's most prestigious and lucrative landmarks.

The Empire State Building's spacious lobby (left) is sheathed with lustrous marbles imported from Belgium, France, Germany, and Italy. Hundreds of firms (listed behind the reception desk, top) rent office space in the building. Technical equipment, such as heating and electrical units (above) found beneath the concourse, provides for the comfort and safety of the thousands who work in the building. Numerous banks, newsstands, clothing shops, and restaurants (below) occupy space on the ground floor and concourse.

The views from the building's two observatories on the 86th and 102nd floors are particularly magnificent on clear days when it is possible to see more than eighty miles.

Above, a view from the building looking toward the East River. The structure with the scalloped crown is the Chrysler Building, designed by William Van Alen and completed early in 1930. At 1,048 feet, the building was the first to exceed the height of the Eiffel Tower and was the world's tallest office building until the Empire State surpassed it four months later.

Left, visitors survey the view from the outdoor promenade on the 86th floor, 1,050 feet above street level.

Right, one of scores of window washers who are charged with cleaning each of the tower's windows every two months.

Empire State Building New York City

The Empire State Building is the world's most famous skyscraper. Towering 1,250 feet above the sidewalks of New York—the archetypal American city, the gateway to the New World—it was destined to become a symbol of American ambition. For forty years it was the tallest building on earth. This distinction seems even more remarkable considering that the Empire State was constructed during the bleak years of the Great Depression, when capital was scarce and confidence was scarcer still. Ever since, the world has associated this building with America's power of renewal, its wealth, and its energy.

Long before the Empire State was constructed at the corner of Thirty-fourth Street and Fifth Avenue, this part of midtown Manhattan had been associated with another aspect of American capitalism. In 1827, William Backhouse Astor bought the twenty-acre farm which was then on the site. Astor was the son of John Jacob Astor, the richest man in America, and a successful financier in his own right. By 1859, his sons had built adjoining mansions on the property, and New York social life soon came to revolve around the lavish balls given by his daughter-in-law, Mrs. William B. Astor, Jr. Invitations to Mrs. Astor's soirees were held in such reverence that New York's elite eventually came to be called the Four Hundred, reflecting the capacity of her ballroom.

The Astors' prominence in society continued unchallenged for almost forty years. In 1892, however, there was a quarrel between Mrs. Astor and her nephew's wife, when the latter attempted to stage a social coup d'état. As a consequence, William Waldorf Astor, the nephew, removed his family to England, where he eventually became a viscount. He also—out of spite, it is said—tore down his New York mansion and replaced it with an elegant thirteen-story hotel, which he called the Waldorf in honor of the German town from which his great-grandfather had emigrated. The Astors were not ones to let a quarrel stand in the way of a good investment opportunity. In 1897, Mrs. Astor moved uptown and replaced *her* mansion with a connecting seventeen-story hotel, the Astoria.

The adjacent hotels, which operated jointly as the Waldorf-Astoria, were frequented by princes and diplomats and pedigreed New York socialites. But despite its reputation for refinement and glamour, the Waldorf-Astoria was destined to be a victim of changing times. By the 1920s, the Waldorf's sumptuous suites and glittering reception rooms were often empty. Fashion had changed; society had moved uptown or to the cooler suburbs. The hotel's owners had little choice but to follow suit. In 1929, a new Waldorf-Astoria was built on Park Avenue between Forty-ninth and Fiftieth streets and the downtown site was sold.

The buyer was the Empire State Corporation, a company organized by John Jacob Raskob of General Motors and Pierre S. Du Pont of E. I. Du Pont de Nemours. The corporation was headed by

The Empire State Building looms above its Manhattan neighbors in this rendering commissioned by the Empire State Corporation for the official opening on May 1, 1931.

The tower's freestanding steel frame was an American technical development. Its strength was put to a severe test in 1945, when a U.S. Army pilot flew into the seventy-ninth floor, killing sixteen people. Repairs cost a million dollars but the basic structure was unharmed.

Alfred E. Smith, four-time governor of New York and Democratic presidential candidate in 1928. The company decided to demolish the hotel and erect a huge office building in its place on the two-acre site, located midway between Grand Central and Pennsylvania stations.

There were, however, several obstacles. For one thing, the cost of the land was staggering—$17.5 million, or about $200 per square foot. Construction costs were

also high and ready cash difficult to come by. Then as now, economics and city regulations strictly defined the form of any office building, while the congested city streets hindered such large-scale construction projects. Moreover, the entire building had to be finished by May 1, 1931, only twenty months after the demolition of the Waldorf-Astoria. As May 1 was the traditional date for the beginning of commercial leases, it was financially imperative to meet this deadline.

The Empire State Corporation had anticipated many of these difficulties, and its well-connected backers were able to raise the necessary loans and mortgages. In September 1929, the company hired the architectural firm of Shreve, Lamb, and Harmon. By mid-October, the old hotel had been torn down. When the stock market crashed on October 29, plans for the Empire State Building were well under way.

The first step for Lamb, the architect in charge of the project, was to find a design that would be compatible with the rigid building code of the city as well as the corporation's precise financial limitations. The size of the building—36 million cubic feet—had already been decided by dividing the amount of available funds by the estimated cost per cubic foot.

The general shape of the building was only a little more difficult to determine. Under the zoning regulations passed in 1916, buildings on Fifth Avenue could rise only 125 feet above the sidewalk edge before they were required to step back to allow light and air into the street below. A tower of unlimited height was permitted, but only on one quarter of the site area. This law, which remained unchanged until 1960, spawned the familiar ziggurat-shaped skyscrapers of New York City.

Lamb submitted to the corporation seventeen variations of the design. Raskob eventually decided on the sixteenth, demanding an addition of a 222-foot mooring mast for dirigibles. The building was to be five stories high along Thirty-third and Thirty-fourth streets and Fifth Avenue, and then rise in an almost sheer-sided

Steel girders made to exact specifications and stored near the site were lifted into place by cranes. Working at an average rate of four and a half floors per week, the builders finished the entire frame in just eight months.

tower an additional eighty-one stories above the city. Even without the mast, it would be a full twelve stories taller than the already announced Chrysler Building. This was scheduled for completion only a few months earlier than the Empire State and was the first building designed to exceed the height of the Eiffel Tower.

Lamb's design was no artistic masterpiece, and it certainly did not rival the more exotic Chrysler Building. Nevertheless, it did contain elements of the new Art Deco style. The façade is sheathed in Indiana limestone and granite, with vertical strips of a chrome-nickel-steel alloy that give it a streamlined look. This same alloy frames the windows, reinforcing the impression of strength and substance conveyed by the design.

More impressive than the design was the way it was executed. Primary credit for that epic achievement went to the contractors Starrett Brothers & Eken and to the engineer H. G. Balcom. While Lamb was designing the building, they estab-

lished an exacting schedule that would assure completion of the tower within the proposed twenty months. Because the site was located in the midst of a busy urban section, surrounded on three sides by streets, careful organization was essential. Rigorous schedules for the delivery of supplies and construction materials insured that items were always available exactly when they were required.

Excavation for the foundations began on January 22, 1930, and by April 7, the first steel girders were in place. Building progressed at the rate of four and a half stories per week, and by mid-November 1930, the entire steel frame was erected. Masonry work was also completed by November 13, all the window frames were installed by January 1931, and the elevator and mail chutes were finished by February. On May 1, 1931—one year and forty-five days after construction began—the Empire State Building was finished. Sixty thousand tons of steel, ten million bricks, two and a half million feet of elec-

tric wire, and twenty thousand cubic feet of stone were used in the building. The cost was $40,989,900.

In spite of the enormous investment of effort and money and massive publicity efforts, only twenty-five percent of the office space was rented when the Empire State Building opened. The building remained largely empty throughout the Depression years, when only the largest companies were financially stable. However, with the advent of World War II, the space gradually began to fill. By 1945, most of the offices were rented, and today about ninety-five percent of the building is generally occupied.

The mooring mast for airships commissioned by John Raskob was never used for its original purpose. Instead, it was modified in 1950 to serve as a television transmitter, and today it is one of the largest transmitting stations in the world. In addition to ten New York television stations, it is used by four AM and seventeen FM radio stations.

A large permanent staff maintains this huge building. The cleaning crew alone numbers over two hundred. The entire building is cleaned every day, and each of the 6,500 windows is washed every two months. The seventy-three elevators with their seven miles of shafts and the 18,000 telephones and telexes with 3,500 miles of wiring have to be kept in working order.

Since its opening, the tower has received a million tourists each year. During its first decade, tourists as well as the numerous businesses in the lobby and on the observation floors that were established to cater to their needs, helped keep the building solvent.

The lobby itself was carefully designed to provide an appropriately spectacular introduction to the rest of the building. It is an impressive space three stories high, with futuristic, glass-enclosed pedestrian catwalks at ceiling level. The precious European marble lining the walls was selected with such care that in one case workers cut through an entire vein of stone to find exactly the right color and grain.

A one-minute elevator ride lifts the visitor eighty-six floors above the entrance to an enclosed observatory. Powerful binoculars are ranged along an outdoor promenade so that visitors may take a closer look at the street 1,050 feet below. At night the scene is especially beautiful, with the lights of New York shimmering against the dark sky. For those who wish to get an even better view, there is another observatory on the 102nd floor, the highest point open to the public. From this small, glass-enclosed space 1,250 feet above ground level, it is possible on a clear day to see eighty miles in every direction.

At these heights, the visitor is sometimes confronted with unusual weather conditions. Rain appears to fall upward as surging currents of warm air move up from the city below. Pollution also plays tricks on the eye when airborne dust particles give the rain a reddish tinge. And the wind pressure is tremendous, particularly during hurricanes. Gyroscopic tests performed in 1956, however, indicated that the Empire State Building—far more rigid than its modern counterparts—never sways more than one and a half inches in any direction.

The Empire State Building has relinquished its title as the tallest skyscraper in the world. Though the Sears Tower in Chicago and the World Trade Center in Manhattan surpass the Empire State in height, they can't rival its legendary stature. For there is a mystique about this building, a fascination that strikes even the severest of critics. As Le Corbusier remarked on his first visit: "I could stretch out on the sidewalk and gaze at it forever."

Lewis W. Hine, the pictorial historian of the Empire State Building, toted his camera to numerous dizzy perches to document the work of the men who constructed the building. Here are some of his photos of the "sky boys" who, through careful planning and shift scheduling, completed the skyscraper thirteen and a half months after the first stone was laid.

Golden Gate Bridge

San Francisco

Preceding page, the graceful, orange-red sweep of the Golden Gate Bridge outlined against the sky and the sea. This world-famous suspension bridge spans the strait separating San Francisco from suburban Marin County to the north.

The Golden Gate Bridge is 8,981 feet long, of which the central span measures 4,200 feet. Its two towers are 746 feet high. The clearance allowed by the bridge is 220 feet, sufficient for even the largest ships to pass safely underneath.

Left, one of the two lofty supporting towers of the Golden Gate Bridge. Each of the towers bears a downward thrust of 55,000 tons, exerted by the two great cables from which the weight of the bridge is suspended. Constructing the underwater foundations of the towers was an enormous undertaking, made especially difficult by the strong tidal currents. The bridge's southern approach (above right and below) straddles a nineteenth-century fortress, visible in the photograph below. Traffic is electronically monitored from a special cabin (right).

Two steel cables support the six-lane bridge deck. Each main supporting cable, with a diameter of 36½ inches, carries its load via a series of quadruple vertical cables. The cables are made from 27,572 steel wires, with a total weight of 24,500 tons. Unlike arched bridges—structures that make use of mass, gravity, and downward-thrusting pressure—the lines of suspension bridges are drawn taut by tension.

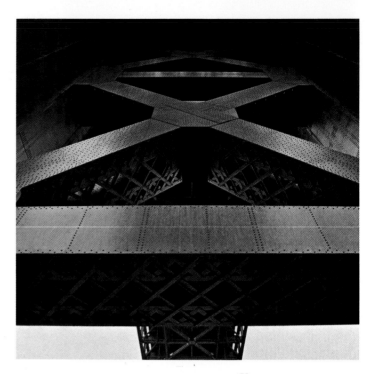

Steel, the material of modern technology, provides the strength necessary to span enormous distances. Crisscrossing steel beams and riveted plates contribute both lightness and rigidity. Near right and below near right, a twisted vertical cable and a grooved casing like those that surround the main cable where it supports the vertical cable. Far right, top to bottom: the summit of the south tower, a stretch of the main cable, and the cable entering a concrete anchorage pylon. Following page, the Golden Gate Bridge enveloped in mist, with the skyline of San Francisco beyond.

Golden Gate Bridge San Francisco

The Golden Gate Bridge is "the bridge that could never be." Or so it initially appeared to the skeptical citizens of San Francisco when the idea was first mooted in 1918. Aside from the projected cost, which promised to run to millions of dollars, the idea of bridging the wide stretch of water at the mouth of San Francisco Bay threatened to strain the limits of modern technology—and the faith of the city planners.

Nineteen years later the bridge was a fact, a seemingly weightless span that graced the Golden Gate strait. Today the bridge is the international symbol of the city of San Francisco. For it is not only a technical masterpiece but also a demonstration of aesthetic balance between technology and nature. One of the world's ultimate achievements in steel, the Golden Gate Bridge is in perfect harmony with its natural surroundings—a marvel of engineering posed between sky and sea.

The city of San Francisco, made by the Gold Rush, was nearly unmade by the great earthquake of 1906. However, with characteristic resourcefulness, the city had not only recovered but was booming again by 1918. Backed by mountains at the end of its peninsula, the city had to cross the bay—which John C. Fremont named the Golden Gate in 1848—if it hoped to expand. For years, idealists and realists alike had dreamed of a bridge that would connect San Francisco with northern California's wine-growing country and redwood forests.

November 12, 1918, one day after the end of World War I, marked the first decisive move toward realizing this goal. On that day, Richard J. Welch, who was later dubbed "the father of the bridge," introduced a resolution before the city's Board of Supervisors to build a bridge across the strait. It was immediately apparent that the problems to be faced were even more formidable than many had realized—Golden Gate bay was both wide and deep, with tidal currents of between seven and nine miles per hour and wind-driven waves of up to five feet in height. Considering these statistics, it is not surprising that the city engineer, Michael Maurice O'Shaughnessy, summed up his hesitations with the memorable comment that it couldn't be done and "it would cost over one hundred million dollars if it could be done."

But one man knew the bridge could be built. Joseph Strauss, who eventually designed and built the bridge, was a small

The peninsula city of San Francisco is separated from the mainland to the north by a strait called the Golden Gate. Below, a photograph of the Golden Gate before the bridge was built. For twenty years Joseph Strauss worked on his design for a bridge to span this waterway—a project long considered unfeasible.

man with an indomitable spirit. Well-known for his inventiveness and tenacity, he had designed more than five hundred bridges in America and abroad, specializing in the design of movable and railroad bridges. His original proposal called for a far more conventional cantilever design—a bridge without cables. He soon realized, however, that the demands of the Golden Gate Bridge project required a suspension bridge.

Strauss's revised plan, submitted in 1920, seemed to offer workable solutions to all the anticipated difficulties. The project generated widespread enthusiasm, and on May 25, 1923, the California legislature created the Golden Gate Bridge and Highway District to manage the construction and maintenance of the bridge. Six years later, the district appointed Strauss chief engineer. O. H. Ammann, who built New York's George Washington Bridge, and Leon S. Moiseiff were selected as consulting engineers. In 1930, a bond issue was passed and construction finally com-

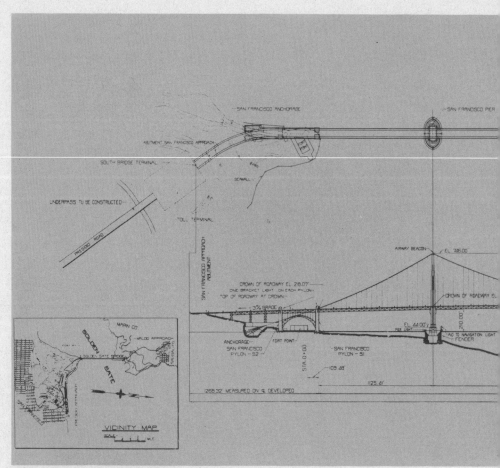

menced on January 5, 1933.

Suspension bridges have been built since antiquity in Europe and Asia and in pre-Columbian America. Iron chains were used for building bridges in the Orient as early as the seventh century. Although these bridges were often easier to build, and achieved much longer spans than other types, they were prone to collapse when they swung back and forth in high winds. In 1801, the American James Finley overcame this problem by constructing a bridge with a rigid deck. Subsequently, the use of metal cables instead of chains to support the weight made it possible to design still longer bridges. As the design of suspension bridges evolved throughout the nineteenth and early twentieth centuries, their spans became progressively longer.

In the typical modern suspension

Far left, the bridge as it appeared on April 30, 1937, after the completion of the roadway.

Left, the Golden Gate Bridge under construction in November 1936, when only 750 feet remained to be completed.

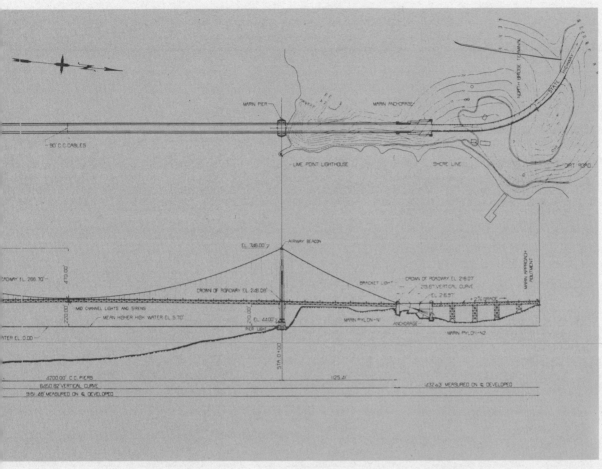

Left, Strauss's plan and elevation of the Golden Gate Bridge.

Below, the famous Brooklyn Bridge in New York City. The longest nineteenth-century suspension bridge, it was the first to use steel for its cable wire.

bridge, the roadway is supported by two series of thin vertical cables which hang from two huge downward-arcing cables. These large cables consist of bundles of thousands of strong, thin wires that have been spun out across the water, one after the other. Strung from high towers whose foundations are imbedded deep below the water, these cables form gracefully curved and precisely determined parabolas. Massive anchorages, usually of concrete, hold down the ends of the cables. The sight of such a great bridge supported by two skeins of steel is as awe-inspiring now as it was when the idea was new.

The masonry arch, the basis of most bridge construction from antiquity to the present, of necessity seems passive and earthbound because it is dependent upon pressure, weight, and mass. But the suspension bridge converts mass into line. The aesthetic effect of a suspension bridge can be as astonishing as the principles of engineering that make it possible.

Suspended from two elegant cables, each a yard thick, the Golden Gate Bridge seems almost weightless. This impression of lightness and grace belies the engineer-

ing and technical difficulties that had to be resolved before it could be built. The huge scale of the bridge and the story behind its construction are equally impressive.

The 4,200-foot central span of the bridge was the longest in the world for twenty-three years, until the Verrazano-Narrows Bridge at the entrance to New York Harbor surpassed it by just 60 feet in

1965. Including the approaches at both ends, the Golden Gate Bridge is 8,981 feet long—more than a mile and a half. The deck of the bridge is 90 feet wide, of which 60 feet forms the six-lane highway.

Over a mile of the bridge—6,451 feet—is suspended on cables. These supporting cables are made up of 27,572 steel wires, each about one-fifth of an inch in diame-

Right, a comparison (not drawn to scale) of the Golden Gate Bridge and other great suspension bridges. Top to bottom, the Severn Road Bridge (Great Britain), the Verrazano-Narrows Bridge (New York City), the Salazar Bridge (Lisbon), the Mackinac Bridge (across the Straits of Mackinac that link Lake Michigan and Lake Huron), and the Golden Gate Bridge (San Francisco). Until 1965, when the Verrazano-Narrows Bridge was completed, the Golden Gate Bridge had the longest span in the world.

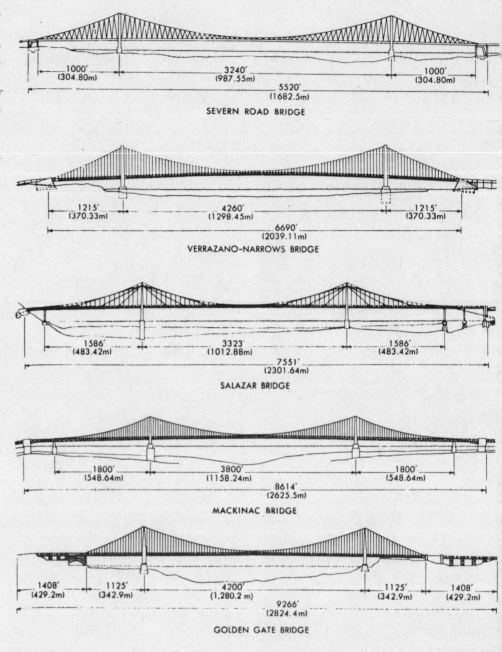

SEVERN ROAD BRIDGE

VERRAZANO-NARROWS BRIDGE

SALAZAR BRIDGE

MACKINAC BRIDGE

GOLDEN GATE BRIDGE

ter. Together, they measure about 81,250 miles in length. Weighing 24,500 tons apiece, each cable has a tension of 16,000 tons, which is borne by the enormous foundations on either end of the bridge. This tension, plus the weight of the cable and its load, creates a downward thrust of about 55,000 tons on each of the two towers which support the cables. These two supporting towers are among the tallest bridge towers in the world. Rising 746 feet above the waters of the bay, they are as high as a sixty-five-story skyscraper.

The clearance allowed by the bridge is 220 feet at high water. However, the midpoint of the bridge can sink as much as five feet below its normal level in extremely cold weather and rise up to six feet above it in hot temperatures.

Several unforeseen events and accidents plagued the construction of the bridge. First a ship in a heavy fog and then a storm carried away parts of an access trestle leading to the base of the south tower, which was being founded on bedrock a hundred feet below the surface of the water. Altogether, eleven men were killed during the building of the bridge; a safety net suspended beneath its entire length during construction saved the lives of countless other workers.

On May 27, 1937, the Golden Gate Bridge was opened for Pedestrian Day when 200,000 persons paid for the privilege of being among the first to officially cross the bridge. The following day at noon, Franklin D. Roosevelt touched a telegraph key in Washington. As soon as the impulse reached San Francisco, the city fired cannons and sounded whistles. Acetylene torches cut through massive chains, and the bridge that was once declared an impossibility was opened to traffic.

"A new wonder of the world is perfected," announced a lead editorial in the *San Francisco Examiner.* The steel "wonder" had cost $35 million, and construction, which required twenty-five million man-hours, had taken only four years—a relatively short time considering that the bridge had been for decades the subject of dreams.

Sydney Opera House

Australia

Preceding page, the Sydney Opera House in its harbor setting. Jørn Utzon's soaring structural "sails," a poetic idea that proved particularly difficult to construct, are a direct response to the drama of its site on Bennelong Point, a narrow peninsula reaching out into the harbor. Because the lively, white sails lack all conventional indications of the size or architectural scale, the building effectively holds its own against the massive pylons and steelwork of the adjacent Sydney Harbour Bridge—a landmark that had been the symbol of both the city and its harbor before the Opera House was built.

This unique cultural complex is composed of groups of overlapping shells, the highest of which were originally intended to enclose the stage towers of the two principal auditoriums. This form was retained in the final version of both auditoriums, even though the larger was eventually constructed as a concert hall without stage machinery. Vast flights of steps (right) ascend the huge podium upon which stand the roof vaults of the two principal auditoriums and the smaller vault of the restaurant.

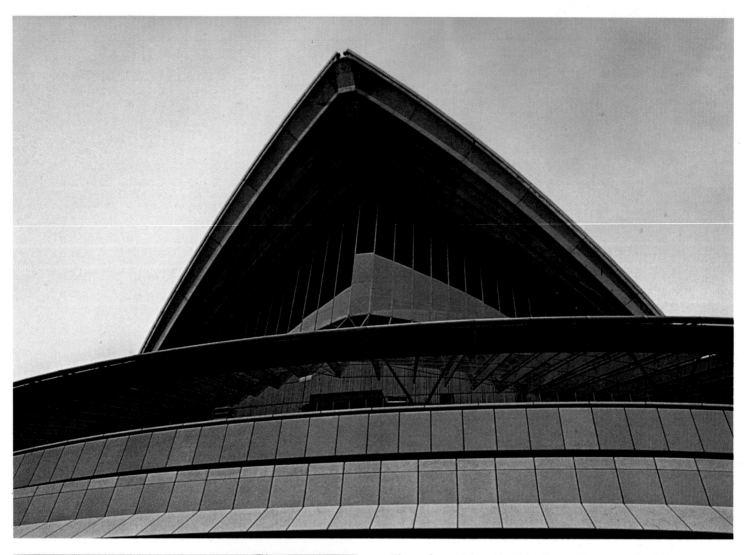

The surfaces of the sails of the Opera House are tile-clad, precast concrete panels that cover dozens of precast arches. Originally the roof vaults were to have consisted of reinforced thin shells of concrete, but the design was found to be technically impossible. The final solution is based on a series of prefabricated concrete ribs, each meeting at the ridgeline to form a huge arch. Below far right, a close-up of the ribbed undersides of the arches. Below left, the entrance to the larger concert hall with the restaurant beyond (above near right) and the entrance seen from the front of the restaurant (below). Top far right, steps leading to the balconies (below near right, above, and center far right) of the concert hall.

The main hall of the Opera House complex (left and right) was originally envisioned to accommodate either grand opera or symphony concerts. It was ultimately constructed solely for orchestral performances. Below left, the rehearsal hall in the podium.

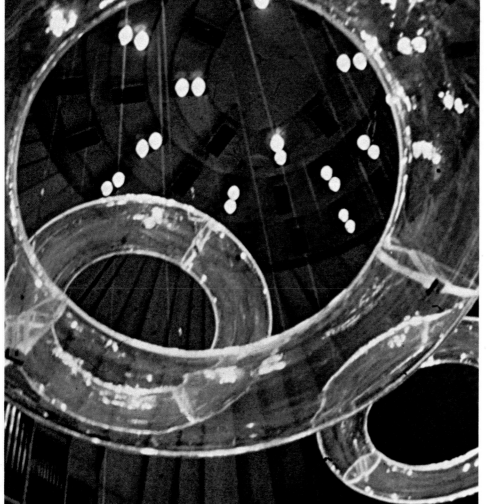

The original architect of the Opera House, Jørn Utzon, was not responsible for the arrangement of its interiors. Because of economic and political complications, he resigned before this phase of the work began. Among the more spectacular effects are the imaginative, vibrant stage curtains (above right and right) designed by the Australian artist John Coburn and the acoustic reflectors (left), an interplay of transparent circles. The seats are of white birch plywood with magenta upholstery (above left).

Following page, the winglike Opera House seen from the Royal Botanical Gardens.

Sydney Opera House Australia

The Sydney Opera House is probably the only building in Australia which is famous throughout the world. Its daring and original design, resembling from one angle an opening flower and from another billowing sails, has become a symbol of Sydney—even, indeed, of Australia itself. But the building was notorious long before it ever assumed recognizable shape. For more than a decade, it was an international *cause célèbre,* the subject of intense and often acrimonious debate. The trials that beset it during its long gestation not only fascinated architects but also stirred the passions of the citizens of Sydney as no other building in the country had ever been able to do.

The idea of building the Opera House originated with the English conductor Eugene Goossens, who was director of the Sydney Symphony Orchestra in the early 1950s and an important influence in Australian musical life. Goossens's proposal for a major cultural and musical center gained considerable public support as well as the official sanction of Joseph Cahill, leader of the governing Labour Party in New South Wales.

An international competition for the design of an opera house was launched in 1956. What was required was an opera house suitable for all activities connected with music and the performing arts. The proposed major hall, seating three to five thousand persons, was to be used for symphony concerts, opera, ballet and dance, choral recitals, pageants, and large meetings. Drama, intimate opera, chamber music, recitals, and lectures would be accommodated in the minor hall, which was to seat 1,200. The jury consisted of four architects—two Australians, the Englishman Sir Leslie Martin, and the Finnish-born American Eero Saarinen. The prize was $11,250 and, with luck, the commission to carry out the construction.

Two hundred and thirty-four proposals were submitted from all parts of the world. Largely on the recommendation of Saarinen, the committee chose the design of Danish architect Jørn Utzon, acclaiming it "capable of becoming one of the great buildings of the world." Utzon's credentials were impressive. He had studied at the architectural school of the Royal Academy of Art in Copenhagen under Denmark's foremost prewar architect Kay Fisker and the influential humanist Steen Eiler Rasmussen.

Utzon had also worked for the Finnish master Alvar Aalto and had toured Europe and America, studying at firsthand the works of Le Corbusier, Mies van der Rohe, and Frank Lloyd Wright. Although he felt a kinship with the Scandinavian tradition of pure design, he also admired pre-Columbian, Chinese, and Japanese formal traditions. Complex curved shapes were another ingredient of his working vocabulary, an influence that might have evolved from his childhood associations with his father's shipyard.

Utzon, however, did not have wide practical experience—he had built very little and that only in Denmark. But despite

The Sydney Opera House comprises two main auditoriums and a restaurant on a great podium which also contains a theater, cinema, rehearsal hall, recording studio, exhibition gallery, administrative offices, and service facilities. The building occupies the whole of the narrow headland jutting into the center of the harbor.

Above, a model of the major auditorium. This vertical cross section shows how the architect, Jørn Utzon, resolved the normally awkward relationship of stage tower to auditorium within the shells. Ultimately, all of this stage machinery was removed—after much had been completed—and the auditorium was reshaped to serve solely as a concert hall.

his lack of experience, or perhaps because of it, he designed an extraordinary building for this unusual site in a city that he had never seen. The practical shortcomings, which later overwhelmed Utzon, were glossed over in the committee's initial rush of enthusiasm for the building's soaring lyrical forms. At this point, Jørn Utzon had no way of knowing that his triumph was the beginning of a ten-year personal battle, which would culminate in a series of sudden reversals, quarrels, furious letters, appeasements, and, finally, his removal from the project.

It is said that the eminent American juror, Eero Saarinen, arrived late at the committee meeting, picked Utzon's proposal from among the discarded submissions, and single-handedly persuaded his fellow jurors to accept it. Utzon's design appealed to the jury both because of its simplicity and because of its dramatic use of the harbor location. The chief attraction of the building was its three sets of thin-shell concrete vaults, a structural device much in favor at the time. Although they anticipated some criticism, the judges agreed that Utzon's imaginative design was important enough to fight for.

The committee was also encouraged after examining the projected cost of his proposal. Their report stated, "we have had approximate estimates made for all the schemes which have been given places and several others in addition. The scheme which we now recommend for the first premium is, in fact, the most economical scheme on the basis of our estimates." Their economic forecast turned out to be a sad error in judgment—although no one could possibly have anticipated that the cost of the Opera House would ultimately rise to well over $100 million.

Bennelong Point, the site chosen for the new Opera House, was a rocky peninsula, almost an island, projecting into the harbor. Although dramatic, the site was small and irregular. In places the shoreline would have to be extended a few feet into the harbor. More important, any building on the site would be exposed on all sides, necessitating a design that would be both coherent and convincing from every possible perspective.

The building's function as a theater imposed its own limitations. The back and side of a theater are apt to look graceless and clumsy. The stage house does not usually need to be as wide as the auditorium, but it does have to be high enough to provide room for scene-shifting mechanisms and other stage equipment. The resultant shape is generally considered unaesthetic, and therefore not to be seen. This, of course, is not such a problem in dense urban areas, where the façade of an auditorium masks the tall stage house from the front and where the sides and the